LANDMARK

CW00569913

Ir

Goa

Christopher Turner

Published by
Landmark Publishing Ltd
Waterloo House, 12 Compton, Ashbourne
Derbyshire, England DE6 1DA

Since 1993 Christopher Turner has spent three months of each year in India. He knows Goa well and wrote the first UK guide for tourists to that state.

This Landmark Visitors Guide to Goa is the author's third guide book to the Indian sub-continent and has been fully revised and updated. This book includes an additional chapter on the ruined city of Hampi.

Christopher is the author of London Step-by-Step, which won the 1985 Guidebook of the Year Award.

His guides to Kerala and Bruges are also published by Landmark Publishing.

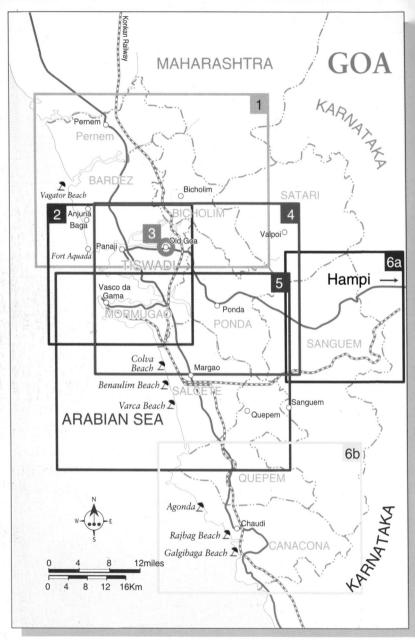

Opposite : Vagator Beach, Anjuna, Bardez province

LANDMARK VISITORS GUIDE

India:
Goa

Christopher Turner

Contents

About this guide   7
Where we go   7
How to travel   8
And finally...   9

Welcome to Goa   10
History   12
Geography   20
The Goan People
   and their
   Religions   22
Industry and
   Agriculture   25
Food and Drink   26

1 Bardez, Pernem,
   Bicholim &
   Northern
   Tiswadi   34
Map   *34*
The Northern
   Beaches   35
From Fort Aguada
   eastward along the
   Mandovi estuary   40
Bicholim Taluka   54
The Northern
   Islands of
   Tiswadi   56

2 Panaji & Southern
   Tiswadi   58
Panaji   58
Map of Panaji   *60*
Southern Tiswadi   69
Map   *70*

3 Old Goa   74
Getting there   74
A Hindu Brahmin
   foundation   75
Map   *76*
The architecture of
   Old Goa   77
The Minor Basilica
   of Bom Jesus   78
Se Cathedral   84
Church of St Francis
   of Assisi   85
Archaeological
   Museum   86
The Arch of the
   Viceroys   88
The Gateway of the
   Palace of Adil
   Shah   88
Church of St Cajetan   89
Holy Hill   89

4 The Hindu Temples
   of Ponda   95
Getting there   96
Shri Mangesh
   Temple   96
Shri Mahalsa
   Temple   97
Map   *98*
Shri Laxmi
   Narasimha
   Temple   100
Shri Nagesh
   Temple   101
Shri Mahalaxmi
   Temple   101

Shri Shantadurga
  Temple   102
Shri Ramnath
  Temple   104
The Safa Shahouri
  Mosque   104
Other places
  of interest   108

5. Mormugao &
   Salcete   **110**
Map   *110*
The Southern
  Beaches   111
Inland excursions   117

6. Sanguem &
   Canacona   **130**
Sanguem   130
Map of Sanguem   *131*
Map of Canacona   *135*
Canacona   136

7. Hampi (Vijayanagar)
                         142

FactFile
Accommodation   148
Climate   148
Currency   148
Customs   149
Electricity   149
Health   149
Maps   152
Money   152
Packing   153

Passports   153
Police   154
Postage   154
Time   154
Tipping   154
Tourist
  information   154
Travel   155
Car & Motorbike
  Hire   156
Ships   157
Visas   157

Index   **158**

Feature Boxes

Feni - The spirit
  of Goa   18/19

Food unique
  to Goa   27

Hinduism -
  a brief
  outline   30-33

Goas' Beaches   42/43

The Hindu
  Temples
  of Goa   106/107

Festivals   150/151

About this Guide

Where we go

This Landmark Visitors Guide describes in detail not only the entire coastline of the state of Goa, but also its inland attractions, many of which lie well off the beaten track. As well as the Goan countryside and cuisine that the visitor will find today, author Christopher Turner fully covers the history and culture – so that even the deck-chair traveller feels a sense of the real Goa.

Most holidaymakers will spend a great deal of their time on a beach or beside a hotel pool, relaxing and acquiring that obligatory winter suntan. As the majority will have journeyed several thousand miles to reach Goa, it would be a pity if they failed to see something more of what is certainly one of India's most richly-endowed states.

This guide explores each of the coastal *taluka*s (provinces), where most visitors stay, beginning with the northern *taluka*s of Bardez and Pernem, and a brief inland excursion to Bicholim *taluka*.

The capital, Panaji (or Panjim), is then explored, followed by the deserted city of Old Goa (the 'Rome of the Orient'), with its great churches, and the southern section of Tiswadi *taluka*.

Mormugao and Salcete *taluka*s, fringed by the great southern beaches, known collectively as Colva Beach, are visited, including Margao, which lies a short distance inland and is Goa's

Opposite: Palolem Beach, regarded as one of Goa's most beautiful, has recently been opened up to many more visitors by the new railway station, a few minutes drive away

second most interesting large town. From here, excursions are easily made to Goa's finest collection of Hindu temples, in Ponda *taluka*, and the Bondla Wildlife Sanctuary.

Two of Goa's most famous sights, the thirteenth-century Tambdi Surla Temple and Duhdsagar Waterfalls, are combined in a one-day trip to the northern sector of Sanguem, Goa's most easterly *taluka*, and a continuation may be made to the Bhagwar Mahaveer Wildlife Sanctuary.

Another excursion from Salcete leads to Chandrapura, Goa's first capital, continuing to the state's finest Hindu mansion, in Chandor, and the Buddhist cave temples at Rivona in southern Sanguem. A return to the coast is made via the only Hindu temple in the Old Conquests to predate the eighteenth century.

Finally, Goa's most idyllic beaches are sought out, located in the deep south, fringing the coast of Canacona *taluka*: many of them deserted, picturesque and magnificent.

How to travel

Organised coach tours of Goa tend to be rather limited in scope and do, of course, restrict participants to a fixed timetable. Moreover, so many of Goa's attractions have an intimate quality, which is easily destroyed by the sudden arrival of a coachload of camera-wielding tourists.

Fortunately, taxi and auto rickshaw hire on a daily basis is extremely cheap, and this is undoubtedly the best way to explore Goa. The younger, or more intrepid, may prefer a motorbike, with or without a driver, but, of course, comfort is sacrificed, and extreme care must be taken against sunburn.

Those who drive unaccompanied, must expect great difficulty in following routes to many of the locations they seek; roads are not numbered, and signposts are few.

Throughout this book explicit driving directions are given, not because the reader is presumed to be at the wheel, but because there is a very good chance that the Goan driver will not know the precise whereabouts of some of the churches, temples, caves or waterfalls which are being sought, no matter how encyclopaedic he has claimed his local knowledge to be.

When the locations to be visited on a particular trip have been selected, it is adviseable to write them down clearly, in order, and go through the route with the driver in advance. This particularly applies to the Ponda temples, which, although close to each other, can be quite difficult to pinpoint precisely.

All locations and roads referred to in this book are indicated on the maps, which, combined with the written directions, should obviate any confusion of great consequence.

The spelling of Goan place names in the Roman alphabet is variable; in this book, that given in the *Tourist Map of Goa* distributed by Goa's Tourism Department is normally followed.

Information about the locations in this book is generally given in the order of: brief history, exterior, and interior (where applicable), and there should be no need for the services of a local guide. However, someone is practically always to be found, in a temple for example, who will be delighted to explain details of ceremony or content of particular interest.

And finally...

Visitors will quickly appreciate that in the coastal *taluka*s of Bardez, Tiswadi, Mormugao and Salcete, where they are most likely to be based, the architecture is primarily European in concept, each village being dominated by its sugary-white baroque church, similar to those found in Portugal's Algarve.

Here, temples and mosques are extremely rare, and historic examples completely non-existent. This is because the coastal *taluka*s formed Portugal's Old Conquests, all acquired by 1543, and throughout which every temple and mosque was demolished by the intolerant Portuguese; almost all were replaced, on the same sites, by churches.

Trips must be made outside these *taluka*s, therefore, if the visitor wishes to obtain a more representative feel of India, which is primarily a Hindu country. A highlight for many is an excursion to Hampi, the ruined capital of the Hindu Vijayanagar Empire, and one of India's most impressive sights. Goa is its closest tourist centre, and as many holidaymakers now visit Hampi this is included, even though it is located in the adjacent state of Karnataka.

Unfortunately, access to Goa's churches is extremely limited, most only being open early in the morning or in the evening. Those wishing to enter a specific building should make enquiries locally. Exceptions are the churches of old Goa and Panaji which are open most of the day.

Although few readers of this book will have the time or inclination to see all the religious buildings referred to, whatever aims and expectations you bring with you, we wish you a very enjoyable stay in Goa.

Welcome to Goa

For those seeking genuine summer weather in the depths of the northern winter — temperatures in the low eighties, balmy seas and cloudless skies — the Indian state of Goa, in spite of a ten-hour flight from Britain, is one of the closest destinations to Europe that truly meets this requirement. Add the superb sand beaches, incredibly low prices, the complete absence of personal danger, ready availability of cheap alcohol, and a wide range of accommodation, and it will become apparent why Goa became the tourist 'in-place' of the 1990s.

Due to 450 years of Portuguese occupation, the coastal areas, where practically all holidaymakers stay, successfully blend a European with an Indian ambience; Goa's generally high standards are unmatched elsewhere on the sub-continent, and provide the gentlest introduction to the cultural shock that is India.

Many sensitive westerners rule out third-world destinations for their holidays, fearing poverty, strange food, sickness, inability to communicate with the locals, intense heat and humidity and beastly bugs. In Goa, they need have no worries.

Although most Goans are poor by western standards, abject poverty is virtually non-existent, and begging, apart from the odd cheeky youngster, most unusual.

Food is generally of a high standard, particularly the fish, which will always be served on the same day as it is caught. Those who have not succumbed to the spicy delights of curry are adequately catered for with European or Chinese cuisines.

Very few tourists report serious illnesses during their stay in Goa; any discomfort caused by an excess of chillis being short-lived and easily treated. More serious problems are rare and usually caused by drinking the tap water, which should be rigorously avoided.

Although the Portuguese were ousted as recently as 1961 few, apart from elderly Goans, still speak their language, but just about everyone is able to converse fluently in English.

Surprisingly, in spite of relatively high temperatures and a marine situation, Goa has very low humidity throughout most of the dry season (October to May). Those who have experienced the debilitating blanket of water-laden air

Opposite: Some of Goa's most picturesque beaches are found in the region of Vagator

in, for example, South-East Asia, will appreciate the difference.

Equally surprising is the relative absence of insects, at least in the dry season — few mosquitoes at sundown, no flies buzzing around the beach restaurants, and no wasps. These creatures are reported to make an appearance during, and following, the monsoon, but by the time most holidaymakers start to arrive they appear to have gone, thoughtfully, into hibernation.

In spite of all its advantages, Goa has still not been overrun by tourism, and those who crave vast stretches of beach to themselves will have no problem, even during the high season of December and January.

The hippies, for which Goa was once infamous, have now cut their hair, changed their nomenclature to 'young travellers' and migrated to the secluded bays at the northen extremities of the coast, where they hold their night parties (police permitting), smoke ganga (police not permitting), strum their guitars and swim in the nude, without disturbing the more conventional tourists or the conservative locals.

The majority of Goa's visitors are now holidaymakers who have taken a flight/accommodation package at an extraordinarily economical price, staying at small hotels or guest houses and eating when, where and what they please. For the well-heeled, there are also extremely luxurious resort hotels, with facilities and standards that match the world's finest.

All are welcomed by the charming and hospitable Goans, whatever the size of their wallets. No private beach ghettos are permitted, nor are buildings allowed to disturb the tree-lined shores. Goa is determined that the natural beauty of its coastline will be preserved. Those who prefer sophisticated, concrete urbanity must look elsewhere.

History

Before the Portuguese Conquest

The Ancient Greeks knew Goa as *Nelkinda*, or *Melinda*, but the Hindu epic, the *Mahabarata*, got closer to the present name, with *Gomanta*. By tradition, Parashurama, an incarnation of Vishnu, hurled his axe from the Western Ghat mountains into the sea, reclaiming land from the point where it fell, which would become Goa.

However, the earliest historical record dates from the third century BC, when Goa formed part of the Mauryan Empire, ruled by the great Buddhist king Ashoka.

Hindu dynasties

A series of Hindu dynasties controlled the region shortly after Ashoka's death in 232BC, notably: the Satyavahanas of Kolhapur, the Chalukyans of Badami, the Shilhavas and the Kadambas. It was the Chalukyans that founded *Chandrapura*, destined to become Goa's first capital, a position it would occupy until 1052, when the Kadambas transferred to the north bank of the River Zuari, creating the great city of *Gowapuri*.

Gowapuri soon became a major trading port, horses from Arabia being exchanged for spices. Arab traders settled in the city, living harmoniously with the local Hindus and being permitted to build their own mosques.

Muslim raiders

In 1312, the troops of Ala ud din Khilji, Sultan of Delhi, pillaged *Gowapuri*, causing much damage: this was the first of many occupations that Goa would suffer throughout the next seven centuries.

The Kadambas returned once more to Chandrapura, but it is believed that their stay was brief as, by tradition, Muhamed Tughluq razed the city to the ground in 1327. About 1350, after much of *Gowapuri* had been rebuilt, the Bahmani Sultan conquered the city.

The Bahmanis were very different Muslims from the easy-going Arab settlers, being religious zealots determined to force their subjects to follow Islam.

In consequence, all the temples were demolished and Hindus forbidden to observe their religion. Some idols were, however, smuggled out of the city and transported to safety — a foretaste of what would be repeated two hundred years later, during the occupation of the equally bigoted Portuguese Christians.

Return to Hindu rule

The initial Bahmani occupation proved to be short, as the Hindu Vijayanagars took the city in 1378, slaughtering the Muslims and destroying their mosques. The Vijayanagar rule lasted for a century, but the Zuari estuary was beginning to silt up, and the village of *Ela*, on the south bank of the River Mandovi, was rapidly usurping *Gowapuri*'s position as the region's principal deepwater port.

A new capital

In 1470, the Bahmanis recaptured *Gowapuri*, by then known generally as *Gova*, and, probably in revenge for the Hindu massacre of their people a century earlier, razed the city to the ground. They transferred to Ela, which sóon appears to have been renamed Gova, and thus founded Goa's third and greatest capital.

Of its predecessors, only fragments remain of Chandrapura, and nothing whatsoever of *Gowapuri*, part of its site being occupied by the insignificant village of Goa Velha, now some distance inland, due to the continued silting up of the estuary.

Bijapur occupation

Eventually, the Bahmani kingdom collapsed and, in 1490, the Sultans of Bijapur became the second Muslim dynasty to rule Gova. Their leader, Yusuf Adil Shah, built a palace fortress there and, later, a summer palace at Panaji, even considering transferring his capital from Bijapur to *Gova*. The Adil Shahs, during their twenty-year occupancy, built a splendid city, with great mosques, houses and gardens irrigated by flowing water.

Portuguese occupation

Alone of the great European colonizers, Portugal had a flying start in early sixteenth-century Asia, the English and French being tied up in wars between themselves and their neighbours, while the Spanish were fully committed to the New World; the Dutch, temporarily under the suzerainty of Spain, were still an impotent force.

Vasco da Gama rounded the Cape of Good Hope in 1497, continuing on to make the first direct sea voyage from Europe to India. Soon, in return for assisting the local rajas, the Portuguese were permitted to establish a base at Cochin, in South India. Close ties with the Hindu Vijayanagar Empire to the east were established, and an alliance formed against the Muslims.

Portugal's conquest of Goa was encouraged and formulated. King Manuel had already given Afonso de Albuquerque the rather meaningless title, Governor of India, when his first assault on Goa, with twenty ships and 1,200 men, took place in February 1510.

The Portuguese were attracted to Goa by its wide, navigable rivers and natural harbours, and from the outset intended to make the city of *Gova* the base for their trading activities in the east. It was also to be a base from where their missionaries would spread

13

Above: One of Goa's most luxurious hotels, the Cidade de Goa

Below left: Colourful Indian clothes are a speciality at Anjuna's Wednesday market

Below right: Girls in Goa wear European-style dresses, not the saris so common elsewhere in India

Christianity throughout Asia. The arrival of the invaders took Yusuf Adil Shah by surprise, and his city fell with little resistance. He died ten days after the Portuguese victory and was succeeded by his teenage son Ismail.

Ismail's Regent, Kamal Khan, organised a 60,000-strong army within a few months, and, after a three-week battle, the Portuguese were forced to leave the city and return to their ships. However, they decided to wait for reinforcements and try again later, remaining at anchor in the Mandovi estuary throughout the three worst months of the monsoon, before sailing south to refit.

On learning that Ismail Adil Shah and most of his army were in Bijapur, Albuquerque returned to launch a new attack on 25 November, aided by ten additional ships newly arrived from Portugal. The battle was over in a matter of hours, the Portuguese meeting little opposition. Most Muslims fled the city, but those captured were massacred, a cruel act untypical of Albuquerque. At breakneck speed, the fort was rebuilt in European style, and the defensive wall restored and strengthened.

Consolidation

After the city had been secured and reinforced, Albuquerque set sail once more to annexe Malacca, Aden and Ormuz, thus setting up further Portuguese outposts along the spice route (Macao, in China, completed the chain in 1557, but was only acquired by treaty).

Albuquerque's last voyage was

from Ormuz to Goa, where he died, shortly after arriving, in 1515. His body was returned to Portugal where he was given a hero's funeral. Albuquerqe had presented his country with a city, renamed Goa, which would remain under its unbroken control for four hundred and fifty years.

Portuguese Defence and Expansion

While Goa's conquerors were undoubtedly brave, tactically advanced and politically adept, it was primarily repeated good fortune that prevented them losing their Indian territory for such a lengthy period of time. Initially, the enmity between Portugal's Hindu allies, the Vijayanagars, and the Muslim Adil Shahs of Bijapur, was their saviour. However, it became apparent that further expansion into Muslim territory would provide greater security, and internal disputes gave Portugal the opportunity to incorporate the *taluka*s of Bardez and Salcete in 1543, thus completing the Old Conquests.

Collapse of Hindu allies

Unfortunately for the Portuguese, in 1565, Hampi, the Vijayanagar Empire's capital fell to a large Muslim army, which continued westward to Goa, besieging the city for almost a year. This time, the Portuguese survived without help from other sources, the heroic leadership of Viceroy Ataide providing their inspiration.

15

English and Dutch assaults

Between 1580 and 1640, Portugal was absorbed by Spain, the great enemy of both England and the newly-liberated Holland, both of which were seeking to take control of Asian ports for trading purposes. It was inevitable that Goa would come under attack from these great powers, and naval battles were fought: only the network of coastal forts prevented a full-scale invasion.

Holland took Malacca and Cochin from Portugal, but lost interest in Goa, finding it easier to sail around the southern tip of India to their Indonesion colonies. After gaining independence from Spain, Portugal signed a treaty of friendship with England (which has remained unbroken) and the threat from that quarter was disposed of.

Maratha threat

A smouldering Hindu force, the Marathas, consolidated under their charismatic leader Shivaji and took the provinces of Bicholim and Pernem from the Adil Shahs in 1664. Portugal signed a treaty of friendship with them, but this was broken in 1680, when Sambhaji succeeded his father and invaded Goa; the Portuguese were only saved because the Marathas had to retreat to defend themselves against attack by the Moghuls (with whom Portugal had also signed a treaty of friendship).

Moghul power rapidly dwindled after the death of their last great emperor Aurangzeb in 1702, and posed no further threat to the Marathas, who mounted another invasion of Goa in 1739. Most of Goa fell to them, but the forts of Aguada, Reis Magos, Mormugao and Rachol held out, together with the fortified city of Goa itself.

Luckily for the Potugese, in 1741, just prior to the onset of the monsoon, a new viceroy arrived, accompanied by 12,000 troops. The Marathas were persuaded to negotiate, but their terms were harsh, a ruinous amount of money being extracted from the Portuguese, in addition to the ceding of most of their territories north of Bombay, for the return of their Goan possessions.

Expansion of Goa

Henceforth, the Marathas were to be preoccupied with securing their territory from the British, and, within thirty years, the Portuguese expansion of Goa began. In practice, however, the seeds for this had been sown in 1764, when the Raja of Sunda, ruler of Ponda, Sanguem, Quepem and Canacona *taluka*s, requested Portuguese assistance against Haider Ali of Mysore, who was threatening to invade: the Portuguese obliged, occupying the four *taluka*s on a 'temporary' basis. Fortunately for them, Haider Ali was soon in conflict with the British and unable to respond.

A similar situation occured again, in 1781, when the Raja of Sawanthadi requested help against the Raja of Kolhapur; the Portuguese moved into his territories of

Bicholim and Satari with every intention of staying put. Further support given to the same raja in 1788 led to the additional acquisition of Pernem.

By the treaty of 1791, the Raja of Sunda officially ceded his territories to the Portuguese, who had already been in *de facto* occupation for twenty-seven years. All these gains, known as the New Conquests, determined the final boundaries of Portuguese Goa, which have survived to the day

Indian 'Liberation'

After the British left India in 1947, only the French and Portuguese remained on the sub-continent as foreign occupiers. The French vacated Pondicherry in 1954, but Portugal, under the rigid dictatorship of Salazar, refused to hand over Goa. The matter was brought to a head on 17 December 1961 when, in defiance of the United Nations, Pandit Nehru's invading forces mounted 'Operation Vijay', and Goa fell, with little resistance or bloodshed, within two days.

The Goan outposts of Daman and Diu, to the north, were similarly taken by Indian troops. Not all Goans, however, were in favour of the 'liberation', fearing the end of privileges, a lower standard of living, and a loss of identity through incorporation into one of the adjoining Indian states.

In the event, most privileges were respected, and Goa officially became an independent state in 1987. Surprisingly, the outposts of Daman and Diu, north of

Bombay, are still administered separately even though, physically, they form part of the Maharashtra and Gujarat states respectively.

Golden Goa and its Demise

Under the Portuguese, Goa's capital had increased its wealth and grandeur to such a degree that the port became known as Golden Goa. However, its economic importance had ended by the early seventeenth century, the Dutch, the Turks and the English having then taken over most of the west-bound trading with Asia, formerly monopolized by the Portuguese and the Arabs. In spite of this, all the great churches of Old Goa were completed in the seventeenth and eighteenth centuries.

It was not, however, the downturn in trade which led to the demise of the city, but plague, which first struck in the form of cholera in 1534. Sewage, which had seeped through the swampy soil into the drinking water, and stagnant pools left by the monsoon proved ideal breeding ground for the anopheles mosquito, harbinger of malaria.

By the late seventeenth century, the population had fallen to 20,000 from its peak of 200,000. Nevertheless, the Portuguese refused to vacate the city until the River Mandovi had silted up to such a degree that its function as a port could no longer be maintained. The viceroys left in 1754, and the Senate in 1835. Panaji officially became the new capital of Goa in 1893.

Feni - The Spirit of Goa

The Portuguese missionaries taught Goans the art of distilling, previously unknown in India. The result was feni (meaning *froth* in Konkani), a strong spirit obtained from either the coconut palm or the cashew tree. All stages in production remain cottage industries, from harvesting the sap or fruit to distillation in copper stills, steaming away aromatically in the countryside.

It was feared that when the Portuguese were expelled from Goa, the new regime would put a stop to this rather un-Indian activity, but the authorities quickly appreciated that to ban production would inflict poverty on many Goans, whose livelihood depended on the trade.

Feni from the coconut palm and the cashew tree is generally purchased from taverns; also available is the less alcoholic cashew urrack. Coconut feni tastes slightly of coconut, as may be expected, but the flavour of Caju feni is hard to describe; some find it reminiscent of tequila.

All these spirits can be drunk neat (be careful), mixed with freshly-squeezed lime juice or with proprietary brands of soft drinks, the excessive sweetness of which may be reduced by adding soda water. If purchasing a bottle of feni to bring home, ensure that it is adequately sealed for travelling. Apparently, well-aged vintage feni is also produced, but it takes some tracking down.

Coconut Feni

Remarkably agile climbers tap the sap (toddy) from the base of new shoots at the top of the tree. Unfortunately, this prohibits the growth of coconuts, but the procedure may be reversed at any time. A high yield is obtained, tapping being possible every few weeks throughout the year. However, in the monsoon period, the trunks become slippery and too dangerous to climb.

Every tapper is licensed, and his number is indicated on all the trees that he is permitted to tap. Toddy, innocuous and slightly sweet, is pleasant enough when drunk shortly after it has been tapped, but it soon begins to ferment, developing an unpleasant, yeasty flavour. The brew is then strained, boiled and the first fermentation takes place, producing urrack. Coconut urrack is rarely sold, practically all of it being given a second distillation, to produce feni.

Caju (Cashew) Feni

The cashew tree is not indigenous to India, but was introduced from Brazil by the Portuguese. Unlike the coconut palm, it is the juice of the fruit, not the sap of the tree itself, that provides the liquid that is used for distillation. As, uniquely, the fruit grows beside the nut, not around it, cashew nut production is unaffected; this is fortunate, as it is Goa's most profitable export crop. Both the fruit and the nut may be gathered only in the period between March and June.

The fruit is yellow and bitter to the taste, only pigs will eat it — but then, Goan pigs will not turn up their snouts at anything. Many production units have now installed presses, although it is not uncommon to see Goans treading the fruit to extract the juice in a manner reminiscent of wine producers from southern Europe.

Geography

Goa forms a narrow strip of land on the west coast of India, approximately 400 kilometres south of Bombay, well within the Tropic of Cancer. It lies a little further south than Jamaica or Acapulco, and fractionally north of Bangkok and Gambia.

One of India's smallest states, Goa is approximately 100km (160 miles) long and 50km (80 miles) wide. Its coastline, mostly fringed by long sandy beaches, is indented by five wide estuaries, some of which can still only be crossed by ferries.

All Goa's rivers flow to these estuaries from the Sahyadri mountains, which run north to south, forming part of the Western Ghat range, and acting as a natural barrier to the flat Deccan plain to

Great Churches, Conversion and Repression

Churches were built in Goa soon after the city of *Gova* had been taken for the second time. It was stipulated that they should all be painted white externally, and no other white buildings were permitted. Franciscans quickly arrived, bent on missionary work, and, in 1540, representatives of other religious orders joined them, including, in 1542, Goa's most famous missionary of all, the Spanish Jesuit priest Francis Xavier, later to be canonized.

In the same year, the order went out to destroy all non-Christian religious buildings throughout Goa, and three centuries of religious persecution began. The Inquisition arrived in 1560 to give teeth to the enforced conversion of the local people, and, although officially suppressed in 1774, retained some powers until 1812.

Between 1759 and 1773, the Jesuits were banished from Goa, and, in 1835, members of most other religious orders were also required to leave.

By 1833, freedom of worship had officially been restored to the Hindus, although this had been tacitly permitted in the Old Conquests for some time. In the New Conquests, not acquired until the eighteenth century, although conversion to Christianity was attempted, other religions were not proscribed, nor were temples and mosques demolished — religious repression in Goa had finally come to an end.

Animal Refuse Collectors

Domestic animals, which far outnumber cars, compete for space in the village streets — cows, buffaloes, goats, chickens and grunting black pigs.

These creatures perform a great peripheral service to the community, as, unlike their western brethren, they will eat absolutely anything — plastic bags are a delicious treat!

As in most of India, therefore, and much to the foreigners' surprise, streets are automatically cleared of refuse without charge to the local authority! The most common birds of particular interest are vultures and the black-headed seagulls which hover around the fishing boats in the quieter areas.

Within the wildlife sanctuaries, of course, visitors can sometimes see the big cats: leopards, panthers, even tigers, but they will have to be very lucky to do so. However monkeys, bison and colourful birds are abundant.

the east; the highest point reached in Goa is 1,666m (5,464ft), at Sonsayad. High land advances to meet the sea north of Baga Beach and south of Colva Beach, but in between, the coastal *taluka*s are mostly flat.

Laterite Stone

Laterite is the local stone, pink in colour and volcanic in origin; unfortunately, although easy to quarry and cut, laterite is relatively soft and no match for the rigours of the monsoon. It is, however, the most commonly used stone in the construction of important buildings, particularly churches, where its surface is usually given a protective coat of lime plaster and painted white.

Fauna and Flora

Holidaymakers that never leave the coast may think that Goa has no other tree than the coconut palm. It is certainly the most important to Goa's economy, thriving in sandy soil, but inland, the palm trees soon merge with, for example, the cashew, areca and mango. Around a quarter of Goa's land is still covered with trees, in spite of deforestation, and native varieties are now being supplemented by teak, eucalyptus and, on the coast, casuarina.

Many of the river estuaries, with their mix of fresh and salt water, prove ideal for mangroves, some varieties of which are found nowhere else in India. The blooms of the bougainvillaea shrub provide vibrant colour throughout the year and are supplemented by flowering fruit trees in season.

It must be admitted that wildlife is less abundant in Goa than in many other Indian states. This is primarily because Goa's human population explosion was so dramatic, following the Portuguese withdrawal in 1961: Indians from other states flooded in to share in the good life. Since then, of course, tourism has played its part, and now, at the height of the season, Goa's population of well over a million virtually doubles.

Wildlife has not, therefore, been able to adapt to a gradual increase in the number of human beings, and appears to have taken fright, withdrawing to the mountains. Rarely, therefore, will tribes of monkeys, exotic birds or, thank goodness, snakes, be seen by holidaymakers, unless one of Goa's three wildlife sanctuaries is visited. Incidentally, elephants are not used for work in Goa, and may only be observed in the Bhagwan Mahaveer Sanctuary.

The Goan People and their Religions

Dravidians, the indigenous people believed to have been Goa's earliest settlers, were overrun by the Aryan tribe from central Asia several centuries before the birth of Christ. In western India, they formed a state known as Konkan, and the region now known as Goa formed part of that state.

Throughout the centuries, the Konkan people intermarried with Arab traders, Muslim invaders from the north, and, of course, the Portuguese. Since the Portuguese withdrawal, Indians have also arrived from other states to contribute to the stock.

As may be expected with this mixture of blood, modern Goans can vary greatly from each other in appearance, particularly skin colour. It should be borne in mind, however, that a Portuguese surname does not necessarily indicate Portuguese ancestry, as interbreeding between conquerors and conquered was never as widespread as generally supposed. The common occurrence of such names is due to the Portuguese insistence that Goan converts to Christianity should take a Portuguese name on baptism.

In spite of their varying ancestry (and religious beliefs), there is undoubtedly a Goan identity of attitude, which expresses itself in a relaxed view of life and a generally laid-back manner, which strangers find most appealing. In spite of the state's dependence on tourism, local Goans exhibit few signs of venality and the holidaymaker does not have to be perpetually on the lookout for overcharging or short change, apart, of course, from auto rickshaw, motorbike and taxi-drivers, who, as in most third-world countries, must be watched like hawks.

Visitors will pass a multitude of churches during their stay in Goa, but only 30 per cent of the population are Christian, and the majority of these live near the coast in the Old Conquests.

Above left: A single tower is all that remains of Old Goa's formerly impressive church of the St Augustine Monastery

Above right: Anjuna's colourful market

Below: Near most Goan villages, fishermen and their boats enliven the beach scene

Language

The Portuguese attempted to stamp out the Konkani language, a variant of Sanskrit spoken by the inhabitants, and replace it with their own, but the attempt was a failure, only two or three per cent of the population ever learning to speak Portuguese. The few Goans that are now able to converse in Portuguese are, for the most part, well-educated members of the older generation.

In 1987, it was decreed that Konkani would be Goa's only official language, in spite of the drawback that it has no established written form, the Roman alphabet generally being used by Christians, and Devnagari, an Indian script, by some Hindus.

In the state-run primary schools, most pupils are taught in Marathi, the language of Maharashtra, the large adjoining state to the north, which incorporates Bombay. Once they have left primary school, however, virtually all children are taught in English. Few private schools, at any level, teach in any other language but English.

As in other parts of India, several Goan newspapers are printed in English. They are certainly worth perusing as some of the quaint phraseology and unusual spelling can be memorable. Hindi, India's national language, is rarely heard.

Hindus still dominate, as they have always done, and are growing in number. Apart from the 3 per cent of Goans who follow Islam, and an insignificant number of Sikhs, practically all the remaining Goans are Hindus.

Happily, there appears to be no enmity between followers of the various religions, many of them participating enthusiastically in each others festivals; apparently, some female Hindu goddesses have even been adopted by Christians as surrogate Virgin Marys. Major religious festivals in Goa are listed in the Fact File.

Sport

Goans are addicted to sport: football because of the Portuguese influence, and cricket in spite of it; many Goans are selected for India's national soccer team. Fishing is also a pastime for many, in addition to being an industry. Bullfights, Portuguese style, where the bull is never killed, are staged from time to time; afficionados should enquire locally.

Music

Again, chiefly due to the Portuguese heritage, Goans are India's foremost exponents of pop music.

In the Old Conquests, little but western music is heard, particularly at the beach resorts. Goa Trance, a recent development, is a local version of the techno style of dance music favoured by western young people. Its repetitive, electronic beat is not the best accompaniment to a starlit meal, as some Goans seem to think. Nevertheless, there also exist folk dances and songs, always sung in Konkani, which manage to combine Indian and young western styles. Visitors are most likely to come across these during festivals and wedding celebrations; the stately, haunting Mando and the lively Dulpod being the most popular. Ever-present is the ghamott, a drum made of clay and animal hide.

In Pernem and Bicholim, a warlike dance, the Ghodemodni, is spectacular, participants wearing effigies of horses' heads. Those who are particularly interested in folk music should enquire about performances staged in Panaji by the Kala Academy, where there is a large open-air theatre.

Crafts and Dress

Goan crafts include woodwork, terracotta pottery from Bicholim, where the clay is referred to as 'Bicholim gold', rattan baskets and mats from Pernem, and brass and copper ware from Mapusa and Bicholim. Holidaymakers wishing to purchase craft articles are recommended to buy them in the markets, particularly at Mapusa, Margao and Panaji. However, Goa is not really a crafts state and most items on sale have been brought in from either Karnataka or Kashmir (particularly the rugs and carpets). Best buys originating from Goa are food and drink, particularly large bags of salted cashew nuts (or unsalted for cooking), saffron, mango jam, coconut oil and for those who like it, bottles of feni.

Those seeking the picturesque will be disappointed to discover that unlike other Indians, Goans use Roman lettering rather than cursive scripts and their clothes are European in style. Girls wear demur dresses, not saris, whilst the men are clad in shirts and trousers (or shorts if on the beach), never dhotis. Away from the beaches, shirtless tourists in shorts or bathing costumes are regarded as rather crazy. Some more exotically dressed Indians will be seen, most of them come from Farnataka state.

Industry and Agriculture

Apart from tourism, open-cast mining of iron, manganese and bauxite ores are Goa's most important industries. The mineral deposits are found in the range of hills running north to south from Bicholim to Canacona.

Almost all the iron ore is exported for processing to Japan, although it is hoped that a large, high-tech plant will eventually be sited nearby on Indian soil; the new Konkan railway should encourage such a venture. Most of the iron ore comes from Bicholim, and is transported to Mormugao port by open truck and barge. Goa produces approximately one-third of India's iron ore, thus making an important contribution to the country's foreign exchange.

Unfortunate bi-products of this mining are deforestation, scarring of the landscape, and the pollution of the waterways and paddy fields when monsoon rains wash down slurry from the great piles of excavated waste littering the hillsides.

Fortunately there are few tourist attractions in the mining areas, and the worst eyesore that a tourist is likely to see in Goa is the chemical fertilizer plant on the headland of Mormugao.

Fishing, as may be expected, is another important industry; it has been estimated that around 180 varieties of fish and shellfish are to be found in Goan waters, including its rivers. Canning of fish, particularly sardines, is a fairly recent development, as is the freezing of shellfish. Almost all tiger prawns and crayfish are now frozen and sent to Japan, whose wealthy citizens seem intent on devouring them to the point of extinction. Only rarely now will large shellfish be served in Goa outside luxury hotels. Crabs however, are still plentiful and cheap.

Coconut palms and cashew trees occupy around half the area devoted to agriculture, but rice, the Goans' staple food, is the largest crop, one third of the land in the Old Conquests being devoted to paddy fields. Even so, insufficient rice is produced to meet Goa's needs, and, as no more land is available, supplies must be brought in from other states. Two varieties are planted, one which is harvested in the monsoon and the other in winter. The winter variety, however, needs irrigation, and steps are being taken to provide more of this so that yields may be increased.

Tropical fruits, available in their seasons, include the banana, orange (but not lemon), lime, breadfruit, jackfruit, tamarind, melon and chicoo (kiwi fruit), which are suprisingly good in milkshakes. Introduced by the Portuguese is the papaya (from the Philippines), and the pineapple (from the West Indies); pineapples can only be grown in plantations as they need constant supplies of water.

Pride of place in Goa, however, must go to the succulent mango, which ripens from late March to mid June (just when most tourists have left). Mango juice, jam and chutney is, however, available throughout the year. Sweet mango chutney, a great favourite with British curry aficionados, is rarely found elsewhere in India. Sugar cane, only introduced in 1970, is grown on a small scale, and a processing plant has been built in Ponda.

Food and Drink

Most who visit Goa will have eaten at some time in a western 'Indian' restaurant, and the basic terms on Goan menus are not very different. However, names of cities are never used in India to denote the amount of chilli in a curry; one will not see, for

Food Unique to Goa

Ambot-tik — Hot, sour curry: meat or fish.

Balchao — Bright red curry: meat, fish or shellfish.

Bangra — Goa's most popular fish, similar to mackerel, served in many ways

Bebinca — Cake made from ten layers of coconut-flavoured pancakes.

Cabidel — A pork dish.

Cafreal — Chicken or fish marinated in mint marsala and fried.

Caldeen — Yellow curry: fish.

Chourisso — Spicy sausage, like Spanish chorizo.

Gur — Coconut sugar.

Kishmar — Dried, powdered shrimp, used as a condiment.

Mangada — Mango jam.

Moira Kela — Plantain (large cooking banana) from Moira village.

Pomfret — Fish of the flounder type.

Reichado — Stuffing of chillies and spices.

Sanna — Rice cakes soaked in unfermented palm toddy.

Seet corri — Curry of rice, fish and coconut.

Sorpatel — A spicy dish of pigs liver and black pudding.

Vindalhao — (or vindalao or vindaloo) Pork marinated in vinegar (vin), garlic (dal) and chillies. Only found in Goa and completely different from the dish of the same name served outside India — where the term simply means very hot.

Xacuti — Coconut rice with meat or chicken.

example, Chicken Madras or Chicken Bombay.

Most Goan dishes utilize chillis to an extent, but usually reduce the amount for tourists; if the authentic fire is required, tell the waiter when ordering. The greatest problem with Goan specialities is that outside the top establishments, chefs can be heavy handed with vinegar, resulting in a dish that most tourists find unpalatable. "Not too much vinegar" should be requested as a matter of course. The vinegar is made from coconuts and appears to be a prerequisite of the Goan cuisine. Staff in all restaurants speak good English, and no confusion is likely to arise.

Coconuts being plentiful, many dishes are prepared with creamy coconut milk and can be slightly reminiscent, therefore, of Thai, Indonesian and Malaysian cuisines.

Fish of many types are served in Goan restaurants, as are large prawns; all being served fresh from the sea. Unfortunately, the huge tiger prawns and 'lobster' (really crayfish), once so cheap and readily available, are now hard to find outside the more expensive establishments as most are exported.

European-style bread is generally good throughout Goa, due of course, to the Portuguese heritage. Nevertheless, the chapattis and nans of north India are always available, and prove to be more suitable accompaniments to the spicy food.

Chillis were introduced to India's west coast from Brazil by the Portuguese in the sixteenth century; prior to this, black peppers were all that there was available to 'heat' the dish. Curries, as we now know them are less than five hundred years old.

It should be noted that 'meat' on the menu generally means lamb or goat. Beef usually will only be served on western menus, usually in the form of steak.

Drink

The best accompaniment to Goan food is water, which, for foreigners, should always mean mineral water. Mineral water can be obtained in all tourist areas and large towns, but not in the countryside; take a bottle if travelling far. In recent years, Pepsi Cola and Coca Cola have become available and are much more preferable to the sugary sweet Thums Up (sic), which should be given a thumbs down by all tourists.

Bottled or tinned mango juice, although still a little sweet for some, is very good when chilled, and retains the authentic taste of the fruit.

Tea is grown in India, but those expecting a treat will be gravely disappointed. Indians like to brew water, tea, sugar and milk together to produce a hot but sickly brew. Always insist that the milk and sugar are served separately. Also, demand cold milk; this will cause great consternation, as Indians cannot understand why anyone should want to make a hot drink cold as soon as it is served. Persevere!

Coffee served in Goa is similar to that generally served in England: instant, weak and tasteless.

Lassi, a drink made from yoghurt, is not as commonly available in Goa as in, for example, northern India. It can be served salted as an accompaniment to food, or sweetened as a dessert or a refreshing drink. In top hotels and restaurants Lassi may be served chilled, but be sure to insist that no ice is put in this or any other drink unless it is made from filtered water (ice made from untreated water harbours bacteria).

Alcoholic drinks most commonly found in Goa are feni, beer and rum. Kingfisher beer comes in large bottles only and is gassy and weak. King's beer, rather better, comes in smaller bottles, has more flavour and is less gassy. Preferable, and recently introduced, are Haake Beck and Belo (in cans only).

Indian rum is acceptable, Royal Treasure being the best white variety available. Like all spirits in Goa, it is measured in 'fingers'; one finger approximately equals an English triple.

Lovers of English gin and Scotch whisky should make their duty free supplies last as long as possible, local versions being rather different primarily because all spirits are based on distilled sugar mollasses.

Wine, surprisingly, is also available, manufactured from grapes grown in Hyderabad and Bangalore. The 'dry' white is not too bad if well chilled, but the red porto is a poor imitation of Portuguese port, having a strangely caramelized flavour.

Restaurants in Goa

Most holidaymakers will dine on or near the coast, either in resort hotels or private restaurants, some being beach bar/restaurants in temporary buildings, often sited on the sand itself. In spite of health warnings posted by some of the large hotels, there is no need to avoid the cheaper restaurants on principle, the fish, in particular, will be equally fresh however much is paid. As has been said, however, tiger prawns and lobsters will only usually be available at the better class establishments. In 1997, virtually all the established beach shacks closed, following a licensing dispute with the authorities. Their replacements the following year were far less numerous and the future situation is unclear.

Many restaurants will be willing to prepare Goan specialities, in the authentic manner, for customers who give a day's notice in advance. Panaji and Margao have several good restaurants, where most customers will be Goans, and the food, therefore, has not been adapted for tourists' sensitive palates.

With few exceptions, in outlying districts, and throughout Canacona *taluka,* apart from Palolem, restaurants are either non-existent or not up to western standards, so be sure to take a packed meal.

A word of warning. Those who are residing at five-star hotels, and those who propose to visit their dining rooms, should bear in mind that an Indian government 'luxury' tax of 20 per cent will be added to all services which they offer, including food and drink. To avoid a nasty shock, check in advance if this applies.

Hinduism - a brief outline

Many westerners come into contact with Hinduism for the first time during their holiday in Goa, where two-thirds of the population is Hindu. It is one of the most complicated of the world's great religions, and a much study and tuition is necessary before it can be properly understood.

Hinduism evolved from Vedism, a form of nature worship introduced by the Indo/Europeans to the Indus valley (now in Pakistan) when they settled there about 1,200BC. Although it is supported by many holy books, which are primarily narratives of epic events, Hinduism is not a doctrinaire religion, and no all-powerful body exists to pronounce dogma.

Because of this, Hindus are eclectic, tolerant, and wide-ranging in their beliefs. To precisely define a Hindu is, therefore, impossible; many followers claim that Hinduism is more a philosophy than a religion in the accepted sense. **Hindi,** incidentally, is the name of India's official language and not directly connected with any religion.

Most non-Hindus are surprised to discover that, in spite of numerous 'gods', Hinduism is, like Judaism, Christianity and Muhammedism, a monotheistic religion. **Brahmin**, The Almighty, is revered as 'one that is the all', and the gods that Hindus worship represent different aspects of him. Similarity with the adoration exhibited by Roman Catholics for their patron saints has been noted.

The trinity of primary gods comprises: **Brahma** the creator (not to be confused with Brahmin), **Vishnu** the preserver, **Shiva** the destroyer and reproducer. When represented in human form, each has four arms.

Brahma

Although Brahma is always depicted somewhere in Vishnu and Shiva temples, few temples are primarily dedicated to him, probably because his work as creator of the world is finished; one temple in Goa, however, possesses an ancient figure of this four-headed god, which is worshipped in a subsidiary shrine. Brahma's consort, Saraswati, goddess of learning, is also depicted with four arms; she rides a peacock, and holds a *vina* (musical instrument).

Vishnu

Vishnu as himself rather than one of his earthly incarnations is usually shown bearing a quoit and a conch shell; occasionally he holds a club and a lotus flower in his other hands. A more complex, but popular, depiction of Vishnu illustrates him floating on the ocean, his vessel formed of coiled serpents; Brahma emerges from a lotus blossom growing from the god's navel.

Laxmi (or Lakshmi), Vishnu's consort, sits at his feet; she is the goddess of wealth, and was created from the ocean.

Closely associated with Vishnu is his vehicle, the half man/half bird Garuda. Vishnu is accredited with nine incarnations on earth (*avatars*); in chronological order these are: **Matsya** the fish, **Kurma** the tortoise, **Varaha** the boar, **Narasimha** the man/lion, **Yamana** the dwarf, **Parashurama**, **Rama**, **Krishna** and **Buddha**; his tenth incarnation, that of **Kalki**, is yet to come.

The belief that Vishnu's last earthly appearance was as the Buddha (Siddhartha Gautama) about 500BC, neatly links Hinduism and Buddhism. Followers of Vishnu are known as Vaishnavites.

Throughout India, Vishnu is primarily worshipped in two of his earthly incarnations: Krishna and Rama. Krishna's life is documented towards the end of *The Mahabharata* epic. When depicted, he is blue in colour, which is why birds with blue plumage, such as pigeons and peacocks, are regarded as sacred. Krishna is often shown trampling serpents and playing a flute or holding a lotus blossom.

Vishnu, as Rama, is the subject of the epic poem *The Ramayana*; he is usually shown carrying a bow and a sheaf of arrows. The monkey Hanuman, who assisted Rama, generally appears in Vishnu temples as a secondary god.

Shiva

Most temples in Goa are dedicated to Shiva in his various forms. As the member of the trinity of gods who has the powers of destruction and reproduction, Shiva (meaning auspicious) inspires great awe and trepidation amongst Hindus, who therefore wish to placate and please him. By tradition, he dwells in the Himalayas.

When depicted in human form, Shiva has a third eye and wears a tiger skin; he may be holding an antelope, a trident, a noose or a drum. More commonly, Shiva is symbolized by a *lingam*, usually a carved block of stone. This takes the form of a phallus, a reference to the god's reproductive powers.

In Goa, Shiva is sometimes depicted as the terrifying **Betal**, draped with human skulls; a scorpion sits on his stomach. Shiva's vehicle, the bull **Nandi** (joyous), normally guards the shrine in Shiva temples. Followers of Shiva are known as Shaivites.

(cont'd)

Hinduism - a brief outline

Parvati, goddess of beauty, and Shiva's consort, is the most revered of all Hindu goddesses. In her form as Durga, ten-armed and riding a tiger, or as the even more terrible Kali, with a protruding tongue and demonic appearance, she is also the most feared, and inspired the murderous thugee cult of the nineteenth century. It appears that Parvati now accepts more responsibility for cosmic violence than Shiva himself.

Shiva and Parvati have two children: **Kartikkhaya**, god of war, whose vehicle is a peacock, and **Ganesh** (or Ganpati), the elephant-headed god of learning, whose vehicle is a large rat.

Ganesh, with his endearing, slightly comical appearance, is the best-loved of all the gods. He possesses none of the violent traits of his parents or brother, preferring to pacifically eat the sweets and fruits of which he is so fond, and with which his followers so liberally provide him.

It is said that Shiva, returning to Parvati after a long absence, surprised her in the company of a young man, whom he failed to recognise as their son, and in a jealous rage decapitated him. On discovering his tragic error, Shiva was only able to replace the head of Ganesh with that of the next creature that he saw – it was an elephant.

Re-incarnation

A precept of most Hindus is that all creatures are reborn continuously until a perfect life has been led. The form of each reincarnation may be higher or lower, depending on the deeds performed in the previous existence. *Moksha*, the reward for a perfect life, is relief from this onerous cycle, ie non-existence.

A similar reward (*nirvana*) is sought by Buddhists, but it seems a strange aim to the followers of the world's other major religions, all of whom believe that there is only one life on this earth, which will be followed, at least for the virtuous, by an eternity in paradise. A goal of non-existence seems equally surprising to those atheists and agnostics who expect it, no matter how well they have lived, but would prefer, in their heart of hearts, not to be totally extinguished.

The caste system

Events and moral codes are believed to be established by a universal law (dhurma), which all Hindus must accept. Every Hindu is born into one of four main castes; Brahmins, the priests; Kshatriyas, the military and rulers; Vaisyas, the tradesmen and farmers; Sudras, the artisans.

Those without caste, the Harijans (the untouchables), are still generally regarded as unsuited for any but the meanest of tasks, even though the law of India now expressly forbids discrimination. It is believed that membership of a caste is divinely ordered and cannot be changed; intermarriage between castes, although legally permitted, is rare.

Hindu beliefs

Hindus hold all life sacred, and many are therefore vegetarians; the cow, as provider of milk to human children, being particularly sacrosanct. A devout Hindu would not kill a poisonous snake, even if it had bitten his child!

Cremation, rather than burial, is virtually universal for Hindus, and their ashes, whenever possible, are scattered on sacred waters, such as those of the River Ganges. Pilgrimages are also made to these holy watering places, as it is believed that by bathing in them the soul as well as the body is cleansed. The accredited curative powers of the waters when drunk are a further reason for pilgrimages — pollution dangers notwithstanding.

Signs and symbols

Males who wear the *tilak*, a red spot marked on the centre of the forehead, are usually members of the Brahmin caste, but those from other castes may also wear it, and often do so, just for good luck. When a female wears the *tilak* it indicates that she is married and her husband is alive.

The swastika emblem is associated with Hinduism as a sign of good fortune, but it is also important to Buddhists and Jains. When the top bar faces right, the swastika symbolizes the day, when it faces left, the night; only rarely will the swastika be seen in the latter style. On its formation in 1919, the German Nazi Party adopted the swastika as its emblem (the top bar facing right), and in 1935 it was made Germany's national flag.

A good introduction for those who wish to learn more about this ancient religion is the book *Hinduism* by K. M. Sen (Penguin, 1961). Although it is not possible to become a Hindu by conversion, only by birth, westerners are able to seek spiritual guidance from a guru.

In Goa, it will be noted that, as in other parts of India, there are names for gods which are specific to an area. A few of the gods are unique, but most will simply be variants on, or combinations of, those referred to above.

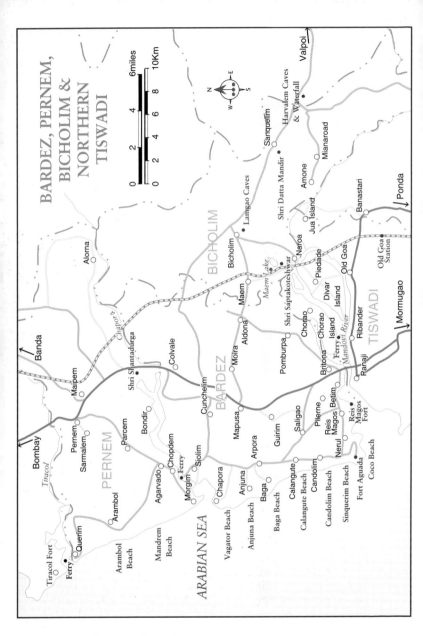

Opposite: *Baga Beach, Bardez*

Bardez, Pernem, Bicholim & Northern Tiswadi

The Northern Beaches

The beaches of Bardez, from Fort Aguada to Baga, are primarily favoured by package tourists, while those of Pernem, due to difficulty of access and the limited top class accommodation available, generally remain the preserve of young travellers. However, trains on the new Konkan railway will stop at Pernem town, greatly facilitating access to the area, and the situation may then change.

From Fort Aguada northward, the road linking the villages of Candolim, Calangute and Baga runs almost half a mile inland for most of its route, and much of north Goa's tourist accommodation is to be found along this stretch.

If travelling between Fort Aguada and Baga by bus, it is necessary to change vehicles at Calangute in order to complete the journey. Although fares are low, the buses progress agonisingly slowly along most of the route. Drivers searchingly peruse both sides of the road as if their lives depended on picking up one more passenger. Most will opt for taxis.

Fishermen operate boat trips from many points; these include an early morning Dolphin Point excursion to watch dolphins swimming near Fort Aguada and a "Crocodile Dundee" cruise up the Zuari River, where crocodiles can be seen basking.

Sinquerim Beach to Baga Beach along the shore

Many will attempt to walk from Sinquerim Beach, below Fort Aguada, to Baga Beach, a distance of roughly 9 km (5.5 miles). At least two hours should be allocated for the expedition, excluding pauses for a splash in the sea or a refreshing drink at a beach bar. Fortunately, refreshments are available at intervals along most of the route, and few will wish to complete the journey non-stop!

Scenically, however, there is little variation until Calangute is reached, as the trees lie well back from the sea, with flat land behind, much of it paddy fields. There are no rocks, and the beach-front restaurants are all low-rise, temporary shacks, constructed from palm fronds fixed to a framework of poles; nevertheless, for those who delight in very long, unbroken beaches, the promenade will give much enjoyment.

Calangute Beach lies between Candolim and Baga and is heralded by the welcome appearance of picturesque fishing boats, many of which are usually being tended by youthful mariners. Overlooking the beach, **Souza Lobo's** is an outstanding but reasonably priced restaurant, while, just back from the beach, **Tito's** remains the area's most popular disco.

Package tourists now predominate, but it was here in the 1960s that the first hippy invaders of Goa decided to settle.

Until recently, beach vendors were a real nuisance at this point, but although some still operate – selling fruit, trinkets and massages – the authorities have at last got to grips with the problem and their numbers are greatly reduced. Most come from Karnataka and can be recognised by their colourful dress.

Calangute Beach imperceptibly merges into **Baga Beach**, equally popular with tourists and with the advantage of coastal diversity: although one long, straight beach stretches southward to Aguada Fort, northward, the Baga River and a rocky headland provides variety.

Baga's own beach is separated from the headland by the Baga River, little more than a small stream at this point, but even at high tide this may be waded, and there is no danger of being cut off. Surprisingly, in view of this stream, the sand at Baga is noticeably whiter than further south, no muddy deposits being swept down from the hills behind. Fishing boats are moored on the beach during the day and enliven the scene, as well as ensuring the freshest of seafood in the local restaurants and bars.

St Anthony's, overlooking the beach, is one of Baga's most highly respected restaurants, and the brothers who run it pride themselves on the high quality of their food. This is one of the best places in which to savour the Goan specialities of sorpatel and vindalho (or vindalao) at their authentic best.

Anjuna Beach

It was to Anjuna Beach that the hippies first moved when they vacated Calangute, and, as most of the accommodation provided has very basic facilities, youngsters (and the young at heart) still predominate. In fact, this applies to the remainder of Goa's northern coastline, with very few exceptions. Easier access, via the new Konkan railway station at Pernem town, may well lead to more varied tourist development. Buses ply between Mapusa and Anjuna and there is a more direct route for those with vehicles.

An attractive footpath around the headland links Baga Beach with Anjuna and at low tide, the Baga River can be paddled across. At other times, wading is involved, or a diversion inland of about one kilometre must be made to reach the bridge.

On Wednesdays, when the sea is calm, fishing boats transport visitors directly from Baga to Anjuna. A return journey by boat is also recommended as the taxi drivers demand rip-off fairs to any destination on market day.

Wednesday is the big day in Anjuna, when everyone visits the small village to attend the flea market, held just behind the beach. However, it is not so much a flea market as an Indian clothes and souvenirs market, with, in the main, the same items on sale from stalls and tables as are available in the shops. Young western travellers also get in on the act, as anyone can sell wares at the market by paying a small amount for their plot; home-made apple pies, for example, are quite a surprising sight on the Indian sub-continent!

Drugs

Drugs are freely available in Anjuna market, not, of course, from stall holders, but from dealers who mingle with the crowd. A few years ago, the market was suspended due to the narcotics problem. If tourists in Goa are caught with any drugs, including marijuana (ganga), the authorities show no mercy. Quite a sizeable amount of backsheesh is necessary to avoid prosecution and an almost certain jail sentence. Goan police are evidently very active in the early hours of the morning, on the lookout for returning partygoers who might have drugs in their possession.

Worth noting in Anjuna village is the **Albuquerque mansion**, built in the 1920s by a Goan who returned home after practising as a doctor in Zanzibar. Its arched verandah, with a terrace above, is reminiscent of colonial buildings in East Africa.

Vagator

Between Anjuna and Vagator there is no beach path, and a steep climb over the headland must be undertaken to proceed northwards on foot. Alternatively you can take the bus to Mapusa and out again to Vagator — or take a taxi...

Vagator's two beautiful beaches, known as Big Vagator and Little Vagator, are divided by a rocky outcrop. Overlooking Big Vagator is the **Stirling Resort Hotel**, the only top class accommodation in the area. Recently however, the hotel has leased all except its beach-front chalets on a time-share basis. Tourists, therefore, have the pleasure of directly facing the sea, but should note that Vagator Beach is a popular venue for all night parties during the high season — ear plugs are essential! It is quite an uphill climb to the hotel's excellent swimming pool and Indian restaurant, but a good Chinese restaurant is located at beach level.

A smart new restaurant, **Alcove**, incorporating Loot's disco, overlooks Little Vagator Beach from its cliff-top site.

Chapora

The road from Vagator turns inland before bearing northward to Chapora village, which lies to the north of its fort, the remains of which can be explored.

Many houses in Chapora offer accommodation, but are generally booked on a long-term basis from October to March. Delightful sandy coves to the north of the Chapora headland may be approached from steep paths. **Chapora Fort** surmounts the headland overlooking Vagator Beach, its ruined walls adding to the picturesqueness of the setting. Rebuilt by the Portuguese in 1717, the original fort was constructed by early Musleim invaders and served as a regional base for the late Moghuls.

Until the bridge is completed, the ferry from Siolim, which runs in both directions across the Chapora river every twenty minutes, must be used to reach the beaches of the Pernem region.

Pernem's beaches

A motorcycle or four-wheel-drive vehicle is the best means of transport for visiting the beaches of Pernem *taluka*, as almost the entire length of the 12 km (7.5 mile) stretch of sand may be traversed, whereas roads to it are few and far between. Buses between Mapusa and Arambol connect with the ferry.

The first section, known as **Morgim Beach,** has no facilities whatsoever, and visitors must bring their own refreshments.

Mandrem Beach lies 4 km (2.5 miles) further on, but it is not until this is passed and Arambol reached that more than a handful of people

Above: *Chapora Village — so peaceful by day — turns up the volume at night for the young visitors that have taken it over*

Below: *The Ronil Beach Resort, near Baga, is typical of Goa's good-value hotels*

Beach parties

Due to its distance from large residential centres, **Arambol Beach** provides a popular location for nudism and nocturnal beach parties, especially around Christmas time, when drugs, alcohol and very loud music prevail. On these occasions, operators of private transport to the beach exploit the youngsters outrageously. Few more mature tourists will wish to stay overnight in the area — for obvious reasons.

are likely to be seen on the great expanse of sand.

Further north, **Arambol Beach** remains the one resort in Goa where the authorities turn a blind eye to total nudism; not everyone, however, indulges. Arambol Beach, alternatively called Harmal, is a wide sandy cove, protected by low headlands. Uniquely, a stream from the hills fills a pool, which almost, but not quite, reaches the sea. Bathers therefore have the advantage of a rinse in fresh water after a swim in the salty sea.

Some primitive accommodation is available immediately behind the beach, but most stay in or near the village, half a mile inland.

From Fort Aguada eastward along the Mandovi estuary

Fort Aguada

The Portuguese erected or remodelled forts to protect all their overseas territories, not only along the coasts, but also at strategic points inland.

Fort Aguada, defending the estuary of the Mandovi River, which flows past the former capital, Old Goa, was understandably the largest and strongest coastal example in Goa. The fort, which occupies the entire promontory, was sited so that its seventy-nine guns would command both the river estuary to the south, and the Arabian Sea to the north and west.

Constructed within the fort's outer wall is the **Aguada Beach Resort**, a luxury hotel run by the Taj Group, which directly overlooks the 11km (7 mile) sandy beach from Sinquerim as far north as Baga, where it is terminated by another headland.

A restored stone jetty extends into the sea immediately beneath the hotel. In addition to providing landing facilities, the jetty formed the base for a cannon, which covered a blind spot in the fort's defences. Apart from this jetty and some remnants of walls, little of the fort can be seen from the hotel's grounds.

The fort's citadel, built on the highest point of the headland, may, however, be entered via its only access point, at the north-east corner. This is reached by taking the road to Nerul village and swinging right towards the estuary.

Fort Aguada was completed in 1617, earlier forts built by the Portuguese to defend the Mandovi estuary at Reis Magos, Gaspar Dias and Cabo, having proved vulnerable to Dutch raiders. A wide canal was constructed, linking the Nerul River to the open sea, thus isolating the fortress and increasing its defence capacity. Although besieged on many occasions, Fort Aguada never fell, remaining a vital military bastion until the Maratha threat ended, and Portugal gained its New Conquests in the eighteenth century.

However, the British were grudgingly permitted to occupy the fort for a year in 1798, during their struggle with Sultan Tippu, who was aided by the French, and again in 1802-13, when it was feared that Napoleon would attack India. There is now no sign of the British occupancy, the barracks which they built having long been demolished.

A narrow bridge across the dry moat leads to the arched entrance, its original heavy doors no longer exist. Unusually, typical Portuguese lookout turrets, curved, surmounted by cupolas and extending from the walls, have not been built at Aguada, presumably because of the excellent all-round visibility of the surrounding area from the elevated site.

Adjacent to the gateway is the former magazine, its structure curved to reduce the target for aggressors. Within the inner walls, a ramp turns sharply right,

a further defensive measure, probably learned from the Moors in Portugal, who never permitted a direct approach to the core of their defences.

The lighthouse

Immediately ahead is the former lighthouse, built in 1864 and one of the first examples in Asia. Its white, four-stage bulk serves as a landmark for the surrounding area. The great bell of Old Goa's Augustinian church was installed here in 1841, before being transferred to the Church of Our Lady at Panaji, in 1871. A staircase links the four stages of the building, within which a plaque commemorates the architect and viceroy responsible for its construction.

A new lighthouse, outside the complex, replaced the function of the original in 1976; this may also be entered. In the centre of the courtyard, steps descend to a great cistern, the excavation of which provided the fort's building stone. Many springs supplied the fort with both fresh water and its Portuguese name, Aguada, meaning watering-place. Now dry, the cistern has a capacity of more than two million gallons, quite sufficient to survive the lengthiest of sieges.

The prison and chapel

A now-blocked passageway leading southward connects the fort's citadel with its anchorage on the Mandovi estuary; however, much of this area has been converted to a prison and is not, therefore, open to the public. Can there be any

Goa's Beaches

The clean, golden sand beaches of Goa are washed by the warm waters of the Arabian Sea. Most shelve gently, but for much of the year, particularly in the month preceeding and following the midsummer monsoon, a swell in the form of a two metre high wave disturbs the surface of the water. This can not only be annoying but also dangerous to poor swimmers, due to the strong drawback after the wave has crashed onto the beach. Those with young children should maintain vigilance.

The long unbroken beaches to the north, between Baga and Fort Aguada, and to the south, between Velsao and Mobor, are greatly favoured by holidaymakers and it is here that most tourist facilities are located.

Between these beaches are the estuaries of the Mandovi and Zuari rivers, together with the Tiswadi and Mormugao promontories, where south-facing beaches and much calmer waters may be found. However due to the action of the rivers, the estuary beaches are narrower and the sands less golden.

As may be expected, Goa's most picturesque beaches are to be found where the high ground reaches the coast. Most of them lie to the north and the south of the popular tourist areas, but they will be worth making the effort to visit, particularly on the new Konkan railway which has greatly speeded up access to Canacona.

Only very rarely in Goa do roads skirt the beach, the reason being that the settlements, even the fishing villages, lie well back from the shore to avoid encroachment from sea and sand during the monsoon period. While this precludes views of the sea from motor vehicles, it also helps to preserve the natural beauty of the coast. In consequence, Goa's beaches are lined by trees rather than buildings, and cars only encroach on the few locations where a road from the interior ends at the shore.

Throughout Goa, most beach bars will provide food of some kind (always primarily fish) as well as drinks.

Long staight beaches

Pernem: Arambol, Mandrem and Morgim
Bardez: Baga, Calangute, Candolim, Sinqerim and Betul
Mormugao: Velsao and Cansaulim
Salcete: Majorda, Colva, Benaulim, Varca, Fatrada, Cavelossim
            and Mobor.

Picturesque beaches

Pernem: Arambol
Bardez: Big Vagator, Little Vagator, Anjuna, Baga, Sinquerim
            (at its Fort Aguada end) and Coco
Tiswadi: Dona Paula and Vainguinim
Mormugao: Bogmalo
Canacona: Agonda, Palolem, Colomb, Rajbag, Talpona, Galgibaga
            and Polem

Calm Beaches

Pernem: Arambol (freshwaterpool)
Bardez: Little Vagator, Baga (by its river), and Coco
Tiswadi: Dona Paula and Vainguerim
Mormugao: Bogmalo
Canacona: Palolem (near Canacona Island), Rajbag (by its river)
            and Galgibaga (by its river)

Opposite: *Rajbag Beach*

43

other complex in the world which encompasses both a five-star hotel and a prison?

In addition to prisoners' accommodation, there is also much of the sea level wall, another lighthouse the Aguada Beacon, constructed in 1890 – and a small chapel, Our Lady of Good Intent.

Here also is the only one of Fort Aguada's springs still in use; known as Mae de Agua (Mother of Water), it was the most important of all, and supplied ships at anchorage with their water supplies before setting sail on the long return journey to Europe.

Coco Beach

The main road continues northward, and the first right turn leads to the villages of Nerul and Reis Magos. Just west of Nerul, Coco Beach faces south on the Mandovi River inlet. It is lined with coconut palms and beach shacks. Here, the water is calm and shallow, providing the safest beach in Goa. It is at its most attractive at high tide when only pale gold sand, albeit a narrow strip, is visible.

Reis Magos Fort

A right turn after Reis Magos ascends to another fort. If an aggressor's vessel managed to pass Aguada Fort and continued for 3 km (2 miles) up the River Mandovi, it then came under further bombardment from **Reis Magos Fort**, where the inlet narrowed. Now entirely a prison, the fort may be reached by following the road to Nerul village and swinging right towards the estuary.

This was an earlier foundation than the Aguada bastion, its original structure being erected on the site of a Hindu temple in 1551. Rebuilt in 1707, more of its walls remain intact, including typically Portuguese rounded turrets surmounted by cupolas. As at Aguada, the fort has its own spring, which supplies it with fresh water.

Reis Magos church

Adjacent, and approached by a balustraded flight of steps, is the church which has given its name to the fortress. The church at **Reis Magos** (Magi Kings) was built in 1555, four years after the original fort; it was soon to be accompanied by a Franciscan seminary of great renown, where viceroys sometimes lodged on their immediate arrival at, or departure from, Goa. Nothing of that seminary has survived, and most of the building dates from the eighteenth-century restoration.

The Portuguese arms and the royal crest, carved on the facade's upper stage, are indicative of the importance of the church. Three viceroys who died on service in Goa are buried within. Delicate Corinthian columns provide the chief vertical feature of the five-bay frontage. Deeply carved lions at the base of the steps, on both sides, are believed to be Hindu work, reinforcing the tradition that the Portuguese built this church on the site of a Hindu temple.

Within the church, a polychrome panel, in the centre of the high altar's reredos, depicts the

St Lawrence Church

St Lawrence, the main church of the fort, was built towards the eastern extremity of the outer defences but far enough away from the citadel to prevent it being used by captors to launch an attack. By tradition, the precise site of this church had once been that of a long-demolished Hindu temple. The church was begun in 1630 and consecrated four years later, as recorded above the entrance.

St Lawrence is small, its plain façade partly hidden by a porch, but it still manages flanking towers and a pedimented gable. An air of serenity pervades the interior, partly due to the softness of its pastel colouring. There are no subsidiary altars within the church; the high altar's baroque reredos incorporates a figure of St Lawrence clasping a boat, a reminder that he is the patron saint of all sailors, many of whom worshipped here before departing on perilous voyages. Another figure of the saint is exhibited in a glass case below.

three Magi Kings presenting the infant Jesus with gold, frankincense and myrrh; the dark-skinned king on the right is very Goan in appearance! Every 6 January, the **Feast of Reis Magos** is celebrated here, its lively processions being a great tourist attraction. The festival is also celebrated, on the same date, at Cansaulim and Chandor, both of which are more convenient venues for holidaymakers staying at the southern beach resorts.

In the passageway north of the sanctuary, a superbly carved tomb slab commemorates Viceroy Dom Luis de Ataide, who died at Goa in 1581, during his second term of office. Ataide gained military fame in 1570, two years after his first appointment was made: combined Muslim forces had encircled Old Goa with 100,000 troops and 2,000 elephants, but Ataide, with just 700 men, successfully withstood the siege for ten months, and the Muslims finally retreated.

Betim and Britona

The road from Reis Magos continues ahead, following the Mandovi estuary. **Betim village**, reached just before the bridge from Panaji, provides an opportunity to visit a Sikh temple (*gurudwara*). It is a rare example in the state, where Goa's Sikh population totals only 2,000. The multi-domed temple is constructed of white marble from north India. As in Hindu temples, shoes must be removed before entering. It will be noted that, unlike

Hindus, Sikhs do not worship idols.

Continuing ahead past the bridge, the road follows the River Mapusa, with, on the opposite bank, Chorao Island. Less than a mile from the bridge is the village of **Britona** and its church of **Our Lady of the Rock of France**.

An unusual architectural feature of the church is that the

Our Lady of the Rock of France

This is one of only seven churches in the world to have such a strange dedication, which refers to a mountain in Spain to where some Frenchmen fled in order to escape the advancing Moors.

By tradition, one of them, a monk, discovered a statue of the Virgin buried on the mountain top, and built a chapel there to accommodate the figure. A chapel was built in Lisbon, similarly dedicated, in the late sixteenth century, and its figure of the Virgin became famous for miraculous cures. The church at Britona, a fishing village at the time, was consecrated in 1626. Our Lady of the Rock of France was regarded by Portuguese mariners as a protector from plagues.

upper stages of its flanking towers are octagonal rather than square, as is general in Goa. The only other example in the state is the Church of St Francis of Assisi in Old Goa.

From here visitors can return to the main road, proceed to Mapusa or return to the coast. However, some may wish to continue eastward to **Pomburpa**, with its extravagantly baroque church of **Our Lady Mother of God**. The soaring, vertical emphasis of the high altar's reredos is Gothic in spirit.

Candolim

In the village of **Candolim**, little is of tourist interest apart from **Our Lady of Hope Church**, mid-seventeenth century work apart from its surprisingly grand five-storey towers, which were added in 1764. Unusually for Goa, their height exceeds that of the facade's pediment.

Calangute

The town of Calangute is by far the largest coastal town in Bardez, but its recent development has been remarkably unattractive comprising concrete apartments with shops and restaurants at ground level. Work has been halted on many projects, resulting in a "building site" appearance. Gentlemen looking for a bargain may wish to seek out the **Benson Complex**. Aigner has built up a reputation for reproducing Church's shoes, made to measure in four days, but lace-up Oxford style only.

In the direction of the beach a small, gleaming-white nineteenth-

Above: Even the small villages of Bardez are graced with surprisingly grand Baroque churches, such as this example at Baga

Right: Goa's only neo-Gothic church, at Saligao

47

century chapel is an unusual Goan example of the neo-Gothic style. Calangute's attractive church, dedicated to **St Alex,** overlooks the main road to Mapusa. An ornamental grotto has been constructed in front of its main façade. St Alex is one of a small group of Goan churches that has a dome as its dominating feature, rather than a pedimented façade. Like the other examples, with the notable exception of St Cajetan in Old Goa, the dome is false. The delightful interior, with decorative shell niches, is painted white with gilded details. Its outstanding reredos, in Rococo style, would not seem out of place in Austria.

Baga

Athough much smaller than Calangute, and in spite of the absence of luxury hotels in the region, **Baga** offers its visitors good food and varied menus. Comfortable accommodation, although below five-star rating, is in good supply, and there is a wide variety of high quality restaurants, not only within the hotels, but on the beach and in the village itself. Most accommodation is sited a very short walk from the sea, as the parallel Baga/Calangute road rarely lies more than a 100 yds distant, and a series of short side streets link it with the beach.

As is usual in Goa's main resorts, the approach road to the beach is lined with boutiques built in vernacular style. However, these manage to avoid the tawdry appearance which has become, unfortunately, the norm elsewhere.

Its hotels will always welcome non-residents to their restaurants, and in Baga three are highly recommended: **Ronil Beach Resort Hotel** (with probably the most spick and span kitchen in India), **Baia del Sol** and **Riverside** (mainly western food).

Casa Portuguesa is a rare Goan example of a high-class restaurant that does not form part of a hotel. It occupies a vintage Portuguese colonial house and is furnished with antiques. One of the longest menus in India is explained to guests by Francisco, the extrovert patron, who will entertain on the guitar when the mood takes him — it usually does.

A short distance from Baga Beach is **Carvalho,** a medium-size family run hotel in the lower price range. Guests dine in its delightful courtyard and rooms overlook peaceful rice paddies to the verdant hills beyond. Recently added is an adjacent swimming pool.

Every effort should be made to locate **Two Sisters**, a small restaurant run by two ever-smiling sisters, where the best vegetarian meals in Goa are prepared, and where fruit juices are never watered down (as they usually are elsewhere in tourist areas). Originally located on Baga Beach, the establishment has recently become peripatetic.

From Calangute to Moira

Just 2 km (1.25 miles) east of Calangute lies the small town of **Saligao.** Apart from Calangute's small chapel, already noted, Saligao's **Church of the Rosary** is

Goa's only religious building designed in the neo-Gothic style. Dedicated to Our Lady Mother of God, in 1873, it seems probable that this church was designed by the same architect responsible for the Calangute chapel. The shrine's figure of the Virgin Mary, to which miracles are ascribed, came from a ruined convent church in Old Goa.

Young boys are prepared at the minor seminary in Saligao for eventual enrolment at Rachol Seminary to study for the priesthood.

From Saligao, two roads lead northward to Mapusa; that which bears eastward passes through Guirim. Opposite the Baroda Bank is the **Souza Goncalves House**, a renowned eighteenth century mansion, named to commemorate its builder, Pedro de Souza, and the Goncalves family, into which his only daughter married. Mass is celebrated monthly in the ground-floor chapel.

Much glossily varnished 19th century furniture survives, particularly in the salon, and is of special interest to British visitors, as its design resembles that of contemporary English rather than Portuguese styles. In 1896, the brother of King Carlos of Portugal, the Infante Don Alfonso, was the viceroy in Goa and occupied the house while putting down a revolt by the Ranes, a Rajput warrior tribe. The former Viceroy's bedroom and the chapel are little altered. It is possible to visit the house, preferably on a Sunday and groups are welcomed. Telephone in advance Alcina de Souza 250635. No admission is charged but donations to aid the upkeep are appreciated.

Mapusa

The road continues to Mapusa, less than 3 km (2 miles) distant. Mapusa (pronounced Mapsa), the chief town of Bardez, is renowned for its daily market, which, on Fridays, is extended by many additional stalls, making it the largest in Goa. Colonial-style colonnades enclose the area. The market's narrow aisles, packed with shoppers in the mornings, are less crowded after lunch, but stalls begin to close at four o'clock. Visitors are advised to beware of 'non-Goan' pickpockets. In general, products are grouped together by type.

An important **Milagrosa Festival** is held at Mapusa on the third Monday following Easter Day.

The town is easily reached from the neighbouring beaches, as there are direct bus services to and from Baga, Calangute, Anjuna and Chapora. No bus, however, links the coastal villages from Baga northwards, a return to Mapusa and transfer to another bus being necessary in every case. As the detour involved is fairly lengthy, it is much quicker to travel by motorbike, auto-rickshaw or taxi. A station, Mapusa Road, to the east of the town, will speed links to the south, as part of the new Konkan railway.

Mapusa's church, **Our Lady of Miracles** (Milagres), stands just over 1.25 km (1 mile) from the

Above: *Just a stones throw from the grand (and expensive) hotels of Goa's southern beaches, the shacks provide much cheaper fare*

Below: *Visitors from other parts of India, as well as foreign tourists, admire the waterfalls at Arvalem*

market, and occupies the site of a Hindu temple. Although the exquisite baroque façade lacks the usual flanking towers, it is beautifully proportioned.

Founded in 1594, but rebuilt in 1674, the church was restored after a disastrous fire in 1838, and again, in recent years, following damage caused when the Portuguese tried to blow up the adjacent bridge in 1961, in order to repulse India's liberating army. Three colourful reredoses within were rescued from an Old Goa convent church, Our Lady Mother of God, and are outstanding examples of the Goan 'naïve' style.

Moira

Approximately 2 km (1.25 miles) eastward is the village of Moira. Like St Alex at Calangute, the façade of the church of **Our Lady of the Immaculate Conception** is distinguished by a centrally-positioned false dome; this example is shallow and dominated by its lantern.

Founded in 1636, remodelling of the church took place in the late eighteenth and early nineteenth centuries. The lower two stages of the façade were extended outward so that arches might be constructed to provide shade to the doors and windows, and balustrades were erected across the entire width of both stages, including the towers. The unusually extensive open space in front of the church is the venue for local celebrations.

Reminiscent of porcelain, the delicately-painted blue and white chancel is a perfect foil to the gilded reredos, which completely fills the east wall. An interesting example of Goan naïvety is the Mortuary Chapel's crucifix, which unusually depicts Christ's feet nailed separately to the cross. The bell tower had to be rebuilt in enlarged form to accommodate the bell from the College of St Solhe in Old Goa, which the church acquired in the mid-nineteenth century.

Moira plantain, grown around the village, are the biggest Goan variety of banana, sometimes reaching a foot in length. Their flesh is hard, and the fruit must be cooked before it can be eaten.

Pernem town

The road inland from Arambol leads to the town of Pernem, six miles away, where there are several colourful Hindu temples and, even more important, Goa's most splendid Hindu mansion.

Pernem may be reached even more easily by the main road from Mapusa, twelve miles to the south, although the distance is longer. Soon, Pernem town will also have its own railway station, which will provide a much speedier link with the rest of Goa's western region and its coastal resorts.

A short distance outside the town, and still owned by the Hindu descendants of its aristocratic builder, is **Deshprabhu House**, one of Goa's largest and most impressive domestic structures. The house was begun in 1693 as a single storey dwelling, which was incorporated in the existing building as part of its 19th century expansion. Pernem *taluka* formed part of the New Conquests, and the influential Deshprabhu family was highly regarded by the Portuguese, viceroys even accepting hospitality in their house. The present owner, Jitendra Deshprabhu must be contacted to arrange a visit (preferably on a Sunday), by telephoning 2912341; regretfully, no groups can be accepted.

Within may be found a temple and, if reopened, a museum. The latter occupies wings of the first of the building's sixteen courtyards. Solid silver *palanquins* (a type of sedan chair), which transported members of the family, are outstanding exhibits.

Pernem's main square is one of Goa's most picturesque, accommodating, as it does, the long **Shri Bhagavati Temple**, its entrance (modern work) flanked by full-size figures of elephants. Bhagavati is an aggressive aspect of Shiva's consort; her menacingly large idol in the sanctuary is carved from black stone.

An important event here is the **Dussehra Festival**, held in the square on a varying date every autumn. It is believed that part of the temple's structure dates from the fifteenth century.

Around Pernem Town

On the main road from Mapusa, to the right, at its junction with the minor approach road to Pernem, a narrow street leads to the small **Malvir Temple**; the final approach is by a footpath reached from steps. This temple serves the nearby village of **Malpem**, but stands in a forest clearing, which is one of its chief delights. Although architecturally unexceptional, a frieze of once charming frescoes within the *mandapa* (hall) illustrates various Hindu legends; unfortunately, only traces survive.

From the direction of Arambol, a turning, right, half a mile before Pernem is reached, winds uphill to the attractively sited **Mauli Temple** at **Sarmalem**. Approached through a cusped arch facing the temple is the Sarmal spring, gushing down from the rocks and leaving pools in its wake. Much of the temple's interior is decorated with graffito, a method by which plaster surfaces are scratched to reveal a contrasting colour beneath. As at Malpem the idol, this time of Mauli, is carved in black stone.

Pernem to Tiracol Fort

After passing the right turn to Pernem, the road north from Arambol village leads to **Querim**, from where, every forty-five minutes, a ferry crosses the wide estuary to Tiracol Fort. Apart from this tiny Goan enclave, which the relatively small fort and a village occupy, the river serves as the boundary between the states of Goa and Maharashtra.

Tiracol Fort, as would be expected, commands both the estuary and the sea, but it was not built for defence against attack from the land. Typically Portuguese curved turrets surmounted by cupolas, guard each corner.

As at Fort Aguada, Tiracol now accommodates a hotel, however, this example is an adaptation of the former barracks, and does not aspire to a similar degree of luxury. A short stay in such a romantic setting is most pleasant, but only really suitable for the fittest, as the climb down to the beach is very steep.

The Portuguese captured Tiracol Fort in 1746 from its seventeenth-century builders, the Rajas of Sawantwadi, who had been piratical thorns in their flesh for many years. However, Tiracol did not legitimately become part of Goa until 1788.

As may be expected, the British, who eventually claimed all India for their empire, except Goa and Pondicherry (which belonged to France), were not at all happy with this Portuguese incursion on the north bank of the River Tiracol, but although diplomatic pressure was exerted, the traditional amity between Portugal and England prevented any use of force (Portugal is England's oldest ally, under a treaty 600 years old).

The most violent episode in Tiracol's history occured in 1835, when, after surrendering, supporters of a liberal govenor, the first native Goan to be appointed to the post, were executed on the orders of his usurper. A century later, as part of the movement to liberate Goa, unarmed Indians made a peaceful demonstration at Tiracol in 1954 and some were shot; a monument commemorates them.

As well as adding lookout turrets to the defensive walls, the Portuguese built a small church within the complex. Dedicated to **St Anthony**, its white façade, peering over the walls, is a landmark for many miles. The church practically fills the inner courtyard, but it was apparently decided that to locate it outside the fort would endanger the security of the complex. Unlike Reis Magos, there was no possible site within the outer walls of the bastion.

Parcem

About 6.5 km (4 miles) from both Arambol and Pernem is the village of Parcem (or Parshem) and its **Shri Bhagavati Temple**. Most of the present temple, although on an ancient foundation, dates from the nineteenth century. Its façade is uniquely flanked by five-stage lamp towers, while the five high arches of the frontage are round-headed, giving it a faintly Byzantine aspect.

Although the main dedication is to Bhagavati, Shiva's consort, the main figure of interest to Parcem's visitors is that of Brahma, the creator, located in a subsidiary temple. Brahma is rarely worshipped in India, and representations of him are therefore seldom found. Intricately carved in a greenish stone, the four-headed figure was discovered in the jungle nearby, presumably a survivor from a lost temple. It is accompanied by other idols, including representations of Vishnu and Ganesh.

In the village of Parcem grows an enormous banyan (inedible fig) tree, reputedly Goa's largest;

while its girth is impressive enough, the hanging roots cover an even greater area.

Bicholim Taluka

Few bridges cross the Mandovi and Mapusa rivers, which separate Bicholim from its neighbouring talukas to the west. In view of this, Bicholim receives less visitors than it deserves. There are, of course, ferries, but the easiest direct approach by road from Bardez runs just north of Chorao island; from the south, the main Ponda to the Bondla Wildlife Sanctuary road branches left, crossing the Mandovi at Bambol. It is, incidentally, in its southern sector that Bicholim's scenery is at its most idyllic, much of the north being disfigured by the open-cast mining of iron ore, which is so important to Goa's economy. Most tourists, however, concentrate on the central area, to the south of Bicholim town, where some interesting temples, caves and the renowned Goan beauty spots of Maem lake and the Arvalem waterfalls are to be found.

Naroa and the Shri Saptakoteshwar Temple

Naroa village is situated just across the River Mandovi, facing the island of Divar. Its ancient temple lies a short distance to the north, on the right-hand side of the road to Bicholim. Apart from a long history, the **Shri Saptakoteshwar Temple** at Naroa, one of Goa's oldest buildings, possesses several architectural points of interest. Neither the temple nor Naroa village stand on their original sites, which were located just across the river on Divar Island; the Portuguese demolished the first temple, re-using much of its stonework to build their church of Our Lady of Piedade on the same site.

Saptakoteshwar is a form of Shiva, and the original *lingam* has survived. Apparently, after the Portuguese had demolished the temple, the *lingam* served as a shaft for ropes drawing water from a well. Hindu raiders then spared it from further desecration by ferrying it to safety on the Bicholim side of the river. Initially, the *lingam* was accommodated in a simple shrine, but the present temple was commissioned by Bicholim's new ruler, the Maratha leader Shivaji, in 1668.

Its stylish lamp tower is the best example of the second stage in the development of this Goan feature, which would soon acquire much grander proportions in the European baroque-inspired examples of Ponda. The pedimented entrance hall, with its dentilated cornice and pilasters, has obviously been influenced by contemporary European styles, while the design of the dome above the sanctuary owes more to mosques.

Internally, the pillared *mandapam* is plain but beautifully proportioned. No silver covers the wall of the sanctuary, which is of plain wood; the multi-sided stone *lingam* still bears indentations made by the ropes when it was used to draw water from a well. At some time, the temple may have been a point of pilgrimage, as a series of dilapidated stone arches to the rear appear to be the remains of living quarters.

The caves of Lamgao

Just outside Bicholim town, a footpath (10 minutes walk) leads to the caves of Lamgao, known locally as **Pandava caves**. They are not signposted, but children will lead the way.

There are two caves, both of which are believed to have been excavated by Buddhists. Both are now Hindu temples, the smaller of them being of greater interest, as it retains a *lingam* and a Nandi bull. The second, larger cave a short distance away, appears to have served as a shelter.

The Shri Datta Mandir Temple

From **Bicholim** town (of little tourist interest) the main road heads south-eastward to the Shri Datta Mandir Temple, which lies beside the river, to the left, just before the village of **Sanquelim** is reached. Here, on a varying date every December, the **Datta Jayanti Festival** is celebrated by great crowds. The temple dates from the late nineteenth century, and is distinguished by a blue pagoda above its sanctuary, rather than the more usual dome.

Between this temple and Sanquelim, the **Vital Mandir Temple** was founded in the four-teenth century, but its structure is modern. Vital, the principal god worshipped in this temple, is local to the former small, but perpe-tually rebellious province of Satavi. Figures of Laxmi and Saraswati flank the idol; all three are of black stone and dressed in sumptuous clothing.

Harvalem caves and waterfalls

After passing through Sanquelim, a minor road, right, is indicated as leading to the Harvalem caves and waterfalls. The layout of the caves and the discovery of figures of Buddha in the area indicates a Buddhist origin. The three caves have been excavated from the same rock formation and are believed to date, at least, from the sixth century; if so, they are the earliest examples of their type in Goa. A single vestibule, supported by crude columns, fronts the central cave, in which four cells contain Shiva *linga* shrines, pre-sumably replacements of Buddha images. Smaller examples flank the main cave.

The road continues to the Harvalem waterfalls, only really impressive in the autumn, after the monsoon has ended. However, the site is always pleasant, with its cas-cade, small pools and verdant sur-roundings.

At the end of February, when the **Mahashivrata Festival** is celebrated, the adjacent **Shri Rudreshwar Temple** is witness to a joyous night-time procession of palanquins and idols' chariots (*raths*).

A return to the border with Bardez *taluka* can be followed easily by visits to three of the islands that form part of Tiswadi *taluka*.

The Northern Islands of Tiswadi

When first contemplating a holiday in Goa, some believe that they will be visiting a large tropical island lying off the Indian coast, rather like the Maldives. Of course, Goa, as a state, is no such thing, but many of its *taluka*s are defined by wide rivers, and, technically, those with a seabord, particularly in the north, really are islands.

When the Portuguese first occupied part of Goa (now Tiswadi) in 1510, they named their territory the *Ilhas* (islands) as it comprised distinct islands, surrounded by the Arabian Sea and the waterways of the Mandovi, Mapusa, Zuari and Cumbarjua.

Chorao Island

Road bridges from Bardez and Bicholim *taluka*s provide easy links with Chorao Island from the north; from Tiswadi, a ferry operates near the village of Ribander, which lies between Panaji and Old Goa. In the centre of the island, the small village of **Chorao** accommodates virtually all the island's inhabitants.

Due to its estuary location, Chorao's shores are lapped by both freshwater and seawater, and, therefore, an unusual flora has evolved: some species of mangrove, for example, being unique in India. In view of this, the island has been protected from development, and a bird sanctuary was established at its southern tip in 1987. Chorao therefore holds a great deal of interest for naturalists.

Divar Island

No bridges cross to Divar, only a ferry, either from Naroa in Bicholim province (a very short journey) or from Old Goa.

Maem Lake

Half way between Bicholim town and the temple at Naroa, is Maem Lake, one of Goa's most pleasant beauty spots.

Surrounded by low, tree-covered hills, the lake is serene rather than dramatic, and owes much of its local popularity to the rarity of lakes in Goa.

Pedalos may be hired at the landing stage; there can be quite a crowd on Sundays and holidays, when Goans like to picnic by the shores. Some food and drink stalls are set up at the road end of the lake, but it is advisable to bring a packed lunch.

Divar Island is primarily visited for its great church, but there are also the remains of ancient Hindu temples to be seen. Two major temples formerly stood on the island, and Divar was regarded by Hindus as a holy site of great significance.

Muslims destroyed Divar's temples in the late fifteenth century, although its Ganesh and Saptakoteshwar idols were saved. The site of the Ganesh temple was later refused by the Portuguese to build a Christian church. It is recorded that Albuquerque saw the original church from his ship on the Mandovi when he returned to Goa, a few days prior to his death in 1515, and therefore, it must have been one of the first to be built by the Portuguese after their conquest.

The chapel of Our Lady of Candelaria

Also constructed on raised land, but at the north end of Divar, is the tiny domed chapel of Our Lady of Candelaria. This not only occupies the original site of the Saptakoteshwar Temple, but much of its circular section is believed to have formed its sanctuary.

As has been described, the Saptakoteshwar *lingam* was saved and removed to Naroa, the village itself also being resited just across the river in Bicholim *taluka*. Remains of the ablutions tank survive near the chapel. Old Goa's pillory comprises two pillars which are believed to have come from the same temple.

Jua Island

Jua Island, easily reached from Old Goa via Banastari bridge, is visited for its church and the remains of an ancient fort.

St Estevam (Stephen) is one of the group of Goan churches surmounted by imitation domes. It was completed in 1759, a late important example, but continues the traditional Goan elevation of flanking towers. As is usual for the period, interior decoration is rococo in style, with canopied altarpieces, Corinthian pilasters, floral plasterwork, and a heavy *baldachino* above the high altar, which incorporates a figure of St Stephen.

The earliest forts in Goa to be rebuilt by the Portuguese were all situated on the islands, but few traces of them have survived. A flight of steps from **Jua** village ascends to all that remains of this island's fort: just an archway, and sections of wall. Views from the summit are extensive and there is a small shrine to Christ the King.

2 Panaji & Southern Tiswadi

Panaji

Most tourists pass quickly through Panaji on their way to see the great churches of Old Goa. This is a pity, as the quiet charm of the town can only be appreciated adequately by staying at least one night. An added advantage of a sojourn in Panaji is its proximity to Old Goa, where no accommodation whatsoever is available. Despite some ugly, recently-built office blocks in the town centre, Panaji, the state capital, retains a great deal of charm.

It is known, from an ancient inscription, that the nucleus of Panaji already existed as *Pahajani Kali* village in 1107. The first

Above: Our Lady of the Immaculate Conception, rebuilt in 1619, when Panaji was a small township. Its size indicates the religous fervour of that time.

development here of importance took place in the late fifteenth century, when Goa's Muslim ruler, Yusuf Adil Shah (or Khan), the first Sultan of Bijapur, erected his summer palace here; it was later rebuilt to become the residence of the Portuguese viceroys and governors, the **Idalcaon Palace**. The building is now the Secretariat.

In the early years of the nineteenth century, Panaji was still dominated by this building, as no other structures of importance, apart from the peripheral church, had yet been built. At that time also, there were only around two hundred houses in Panaji. By 1843, however, when Panaji was granted city status as *Nova Goa* (New Goa) – an appellation that was rarely used – and also made the state capital, the High Court, Mint and Customs House were already established in the town.

PANAJI

60

Mandovi River

N
W — E
S

- Dom Lourenco Chapel
- Park Plaza Hotel
- Mandovi Hotel

- St Thome Square
- Church of St Thome

New Pato Bridge

SAO THOME

PATO

Pond

Bus Terminal

State Museum

Former Mint

G.P.O.

Venite Restaurant

Statue of Abbé Faria

Secretariat

Ourem Creek

Panjim Inn

Boating Lake

Footbridge

Rua P. Nova de Ourem

31st January Road

Church of the Immaculate Conception

Mhamai Kamat House

ALTINHO

Municipal Garden

High Court

Tourism Office

State Bank

Cunha Rivara Rd

Church Square

Govt of India Tourist Office

Emidio Gracia Rd

FOUNTAINHAS

Alfonso Hotel

Panjim Patio

Chapel of St Sebastian

TO DABOLIM AIRPORT

Jetties

Delhi Darbar Restaurant

Azad Maidan

Tandoor Restaurant

Nova Goa Hotel

Goenchin Restaurant

Malaca Rd

Menezes Braganza Institute

Police Headquarters

Mahatma Gandhi Rd

Dr Atmaram Borkar Rd

Dr Dada Vaidrya Rd

Vaca de Boca Spring

Indian Airlines

Municipal Market

Gen Bernardo Guedes Road

Fidalgo Hotel

Ashok Samrat

18th June Rd

Caculo Island

Palácio de Goa Hotel

Goa Medical College & Hospital

CAMPAL

TO MIRAMAR BEACH & DONA PAULA

Kala Academy

Dom Manuel, viceroy during 1827-35, had been responsible for much of the development, and is known as 'The Founder of the New City'.

A walking tour of the city

Panaji, in spite of its administrative importance to Goa, remains one of India's smallest state capitals, and all points of interest can be visited on foot in one day. Auto-rickshaws do not ply for hire in Panaji, it is necessary to ask for the nearest stand. Bear in mind that shops usually close 1.30-3.30p; (all day Sunday). A good place to begin a walking tour is the centrally located Municipal Garden.

The Municipal Garden

This shady, tropical garden, rectangular in shape, is Panaji's most popular open space. The English name is indicative of the de-Portugalization of Goa, as it was formerly called Garcia da Orta Garden and its monument originally commemorated Vasco da Gama.

Garcia da Orta, while serving in Goa as physician to the Admiral of the Fleet, studied Indian medicine and wrote a textbook on the subject, which was published in 1563.

Now known as the **Ashoka Pillar**, the monument in the centre of the garden was erected in 1898, re-using stone from a derelict monastic church in Old Goa. It was built to commemorate the first voyage from Europe to India (via The Cape of Good Hope), completed by Vasco da Gama four

hundred years earlier. India's national emblem has replaced the bust of Vasco da Gama, which originally surmounted the column.

Situated on its hillside slopes, south-west of the park, is Panaji's principal church, **Our Lady of the Immaculate Conception**.

The extraordinary thing about this important building is that it was founded as long ago as 1540 and rebuilt in its present grand form in 1619, when Panaji was still little more than a village with a riverside palace. It must have been felt that it would be appropriate for new viceroys, whose first steps on Goan soil were normally at Panaji, to be greeted immediately with the sight of a major church towering above the Muslim-built palace in which they would spend their first night.

Between the church and the river lay swampy land, some of it used as paddyfields but impossible to build on. A causeway was constructed and the land gradually drained, although it was not until the mid-nineteenth century that the small square in front of the church could be laid out.

Immediately south-west of the church, the **Government of India Tourist Office** provides up-to-date information about other Indian states.

The Secretariat

The road immediately fronting the church leads, right, to the Secretariat, on the water's edge. Yusuf Adil Shah's sixteenth-century palace, in which the

The Church of Our Lady of the Immaculate Conception

The present building was completed when Old Goa's Se Cathedral was in mid-construction, and similarities in style between their façades have been noted. However, the top stage of the central bay differs greatly from its original appearance, as it was completely remodelled in 1871 to incorporate a belfry, to which the bell from Old Goa's Augustinian church was transferred from its transient site in the lighthouse at Fort Aguada.

Initially, it was planned to hang the bell, Goa's second largest, from the existing belfry in the north tower, but there proved to be insufficient space. Before the new belfry was constructed, the upper stage of the façade was surmounted by a pediment, its height equalling that of the towers.

The processional flight of steps, unmatched elsewhere in Goa, was also constructed in 1871. Its balustrade is decorated with a cusped, Gothic pattern, in surprising contrast with the Renaissance style of the church. The architect of Saligao's neo-Gothic church, with which the steps are contemporary, was probably responsible. It is generally necessary to enter via the adjoining building immediately left. In spite of the external grandeur of the church, the interior is aisle-less and the roof remains a timber structure.

In the sanctuary, the three altarpieces are superb examples of baroque craftsmanship, intricate carving on the subsidiary reredoses of the Crucifixion and Our Lady of the Rosary being particularly fine. The only chapel in the church on the south side, is dedicated to St Francis Xavier, its size giving the impression of a transept; this was an eighteenth-century addition to the building. The reredos came from the Viceroy's Chapel of the Idalcaon Palace in 1918.

Opposite: *The Chapel of St Sebastian is the religous centre of Panaji's Fontainhas quarter*

Secretariat is now accommodated, was originally fortified, its defence being aided on one side by a creek, since filled, and the River Mandovi, which then flowed directly behind it.

The present riverside road was laid out on sandbanks, early in the nineteenth century, prior to this, steps led from the rear of the palace to a landing stage. In 1510, the palace served as an important, although ineffective, bastion against the Portuguese invaders.

Following Albuquerque's conquest, most viceroys and governors spent their first night in Goa at the palace before proceeding to Old Goa. In 1759, however, this became their official residence, being known as the **Idalcaon Palace** (a corruption of Adil Khan, the alternative name of Adil Shah).

In 1918, the viceroys moved to a residence on the promontory south-west of Panaji, known as Cabo; this building is now occupied by the governor of the state of Goa and has been re-named Cabo Raj Bhavan.

After the viceroys had departed, more alterations to the building took place, notably the demolition of the Viceroy's Chapel. Between 1918 and 1961, the former palace provided offices for government departments, but, since Goa's integration with India, it has been the state's Secretariat. One of its larger rooms now accommodates the Legislative Assembly.

It appears that little more than the fabric of Yusuf Adil Shah's building has survived, due to its periodic remodelling; there are certainly no obvious Islamic features to be seen.

Although, as has been said, there was formerly a direct entrance from the river, the main entrance has always been from the street. The white roundel above its archway, known as the Ashoka Chandra, replaced the Portuguese viceroy's crest following Goa's liberation.

Statue of Abbé Faria

Standing in the small square to the west of the Secretariat, **Praca Abbé Faria** is an extraordinary statue, depicting what appears to be a supine woman being attacked by a mad strangler. Those who have visited Lisbon may have noted the Portuguese taste for melodramatic figures, which nowadays tends to induce giggles rather than respect.

In fact, the woman is being hypnotised, not attacked; the work commemorates a son of Goa, Abbé Custodia Faria, who was born at Candolim village in 1756, became a priest and later the world's first recorded hypnotist. He spent the latter part of his life in France, becoming involved in the French Revolution, and died in Paris in 1819.

Facing the square to the south, is the residence of the influential Hindu branch of the Mhamai Kamat family that moved to Panaji in the mid-eighteenth century. Their close connections with both the Portuguese and the Hindus made them ideal mediators. Unfortunately, the building is never open to visitors.

A stroll along the waterfront will pass landing stages from where boat trips on the Mandovi estuary depart; these are particularly attractive at sunset.

Further westward, past the High Court (1878), rises the multi-storey **Hotel Mandovi**. This is neither the oldest nor the most luxurious hotel in Panaji, but those who are nostalgic for the 1950s will delight in the interiors of its public rooms. The open, west-facing terrace, at first floor level, is the most fashionable river facing venue in Panaji for evening drinks.

The eighteenth-century **Dom Lourenco Chapel** adjoins the south side of the hotel. Although small, it has two roofs, one pitched and tiled, the other domed. Apart from tomb slabs there is little of interest internally.

The Chapel of St Sebastian

Facing Ourem creek and approached from a short street, the east-facing Chapel of St Sebastian was built as late as 1888, but still in the classical style.

An earlier, west-facing chapel, also dedicated to St Sebastian, in 1818, formerly stood where Cunha Gonsalves Road now runs, and had to be demolished when it was laid out. For a short period, both chapels faced each other. Surprisingly, the chapel, although small, has a nave and flanking aisles, and is well-endowed with gilded altarpieces.

At the west end of the north aisle is a relic from the Inquisition: a crucifixion carving, with, unusually, the eyes of the dying Christ wide open rather than closed, and the head upright rather than angled. It is said that the figure was sculpted in this manner in order to inspire awe in those under interrogation in Old Goa's Palace of the Inquisition, where it originally stood.

On the suppression of the Inquisition, in 1812, the palace was deserted, and the carving relocated in the Viceroy's Chapel, at the Idalcaon Palace; it was brought here in 1918, when the viceroys moved to Cabo.

The figure of the Virgin in the south aisle's reredos is alleged to have stood originally in the chapel of the High Court, where prayers for guidance were said each morning before the session commenced. The reredoses of the high altar and its flanking altars came from a church in Diu, the former Goan outpost in Gujerat State.

Azad Maidan Square

Panaji's most important square lies ahead. Stretching from the south side of the Menezes Braganza Institute and forming the west side of the square is the long terrace which now accommodates the **Police Headquarters**. It was constructed in 1832 as barracks and administrative quarters, and represented the initial stage in laying out the square on recently drained swampland.

Immediately north of the block is the **Menezes Braganza Institute**, which houses the Central Library. Menezes Braganza was a wealthy philanthropist, who pressed for Goan independence; his immense family house at Chandor may be visited.

The institute was founded in 1817 to facilitate the study of the Arts and Science in Goa. Visitors are welcome to enter the hall, which is decorated with blue ceramic tiles (*azulezos*), illustrating *Os Lusíadas*, by Luís de Camões, the best-known literary work in the Portuguese language, and written by Camões while he lived in Goa. Within a room on the upper floor can be seen the table used by the dreaded Inquisition.

In the centre of Azad Maidan Square stands a delightful classical pavilion, its elegant Corinthian columns being re-used from Old Goa's dilapidated mid-sixteenth century Dominican church. It was erected in 1847, to protect the 6ft (2m) bronze statue of the Portuguese conqueror Albuquerque, which had been cast in his lifetime, early in the sixteenth century. Prior to this, the statue had occupied various sites in Old Goa. It was removed from this square, after liberation, to the Miramar quarter, but can now be seen in Old Goa's Archaeological Museum.

A memorial to Dr Tristao de Braganza Canha, *The Valiant Hero of Goan Fight for Freedom*, has replaced Albuquerque's statue. South of the pavilion, a modern sculpture commemorates all Goans who struggled for liberation from Portuguese rule.

A right turn at the southwest corner, down Mahatma Gandhi Road, leads to General Bernardo Guedes Road, on the right. Ahead lies the **Municipal Market**. Shoppers may like to know that the branches of Benetton and Lacoste in central Panaji are the genuine article, with prices much lower than western equivalents.

The Sao Thome Quarter

Panaji's most picturesque quarter lies some distance away to the east, on the other side of the hill behind the church; a taxi or auto-rickshaw to St Thome Square is recommended. The San Thome Quarter is formed by a small promontory jutting into Ourem Creek, at the north-east sector of the city. Its centre is this small wedge-shaped square.

At its west end, the small Church of St Thome, which gave its name to the quarter, was founded in 1849, but rebuilt in 1902. On the south side, the **Post Office** occupies the nineteenth-

Above: Panaji

Right: Portugese
ironwork, seen here
from the Panjim Inn,
is a feature of Panaji's
Fontainhas quarter

century Tobacco Exchange, hence the colloquial name of Tobacco Square.

The arcaded building occupying most of the east side of the square is the former **Mint**, where, for a few years from 1834, Goan coinage was produced before being minted, as formerly, at the Arsenal. From 1865 to 1902, India's British administrators leased the building as a telegraph office. Until 1843, those condemned to death were executed outside, beside a pillory.

Fontainhas Quarter

From the west side of the square, San Thome street run southward to form the Fontainhas Quarter, which lies between the hillside and Ourem Creek. The streets away from the creek now make for a more pleasant stroll, as the busy main road to the south, Rua Nova de Ourem, hugs the waterfront. The most picturesque area lies south of Emidio Gracia Road.

Much of this low-lying sector of Panaji was marshland until the early nineteenth century, when it was drained and new houses built. Some properties pre-date this period, and their preservation contributes much to the colonial charm; very few modern buildings have yet been constructed in Fontainhas.

The main thoroughfare, a southward continuation of Emidio Gracia Road, is crossed by short streets between the hillside and the creek. A footbridge, Rua de Ourem, crosses Ourem Creek to the **Pato district**; it is picturesquely

bow-shaped and reminiscent of ancient Chinese structures. Pato is of little interest, but does contain the helpful **Department of Tourism**, the **railway ticket office**, and the rather inconveniently sited **bus terminus**, to the south side of which can be found the newly built **State Museum**, designed by Charles Correa.

"Portugese " hotels and bars

A short distance southward, on the 31st January Road corner, stands the delightful **Panjim Inn**, which, it is claimed, has remained in the hands of the same family since it was built three hundred years ago. Wrought-iron balconies, softly-whirring ceiling fans and antique four-poster beds greet the visitor to this fourteen-roomed hotel, the unique charm of which more than makes up for its lack of five-star facilities. Non-residents are welcome to visit the Panjim Inn for its bar, verandah dining room, and art gallery. Across the road, under the same management, the **Panjim Pousadas**, a similar venerable property, was opened in 1998 to provide additional accommodation.

Perhaps nowhere else in Goa is there such a concentration of small bars as there is in **Fontainhas**, where the locals are delighted to meet visitors and show-off their English. Panaji, not being a beach resort, is far less inundated with tourists, and chances are that no other foreigners will be in the bar. Take care, however, the hospitality and strong local brews can be beguiling.

A direct return to the centre of Panaji may be made by crossing the intervening hill via Emidio Gracia Road. From the summit, views over the River Mandovi are still fine, but less attractive than erstwhile, due to the concrete multi-storey blocks which now obtrude. The road terminates at the Municipal Gardens.

Miramar Beach

Those who wish to see Panaji's own beach must continue westward, following the main road skirting the Mandovi. Once known as Gaspar Dias, after a wealthy landowner, Panaji's Miramar Beach now commemorates a large hotel which formerly stood there.

The beach serves as a popular centre for locals to take the air, particularly in the evenings and at weekends; the Goans' enthusiasm for football will be demonstrated on the wide stretch of sand. There are also amusements for children, and, of course, stallholders purveying food and drink.

One thing that Miramar Beach no longer provides, however, is sea bathing, the water here having become too polluted.

Overlooking the beach, a sculpture represents Hindu-Christian Unity. Its base formerly supported the Albuquerque monument after it had been removed from central Panaji; the monument has been transferred to Old Goa's Archaeological Museum. There are no remaining traces of Gaspar Dias Fort, which once stood nearby.

At the end of February, a three day carnival, **Intruz**, takes place throughout Panaji, beginning on the last Saturday. Most hotels will be full.

Eating out

Rather surprisingly, when the residents of Panaji eat out locally they tend to prefer non-Goan food, and many of the best restaurants, therefore, specialize in cooking from other regions of India. Hotel Venite, at 31 January Road (its north end), in Fontainhas, is popular with tourists, paticularly the seafood. However it's chips with everything, unless rice is specified. The Mandovi Hotel's restaurant provides genuine Goan cuisine, whilst the North Indian food of the Delhi Darbar restaurant, to its rear, is outstanding. Splendid Chinese dishes, considered the best in Goa, are served at Goenchin, off Dr Dada Vaidya Road, while the Arona Hotel incorporates a tandoori restaurant. As may be expected, the New Punjab Restaurant serves Punjabi dishes.

Southern Tiswadi

For Panaji's nearest bathing beach, it is necessary to continue southward past the headland of **Cabo Raj Bhavan**, which separates Miramar Beach and Dona Paula Beach. On the headland stands the **Cabo Palace**, originally a Franciscan convent, which became the viceroys' palace in 1918. As this is now occupied by the Governor of Goa it may only be visited by special arrangement.

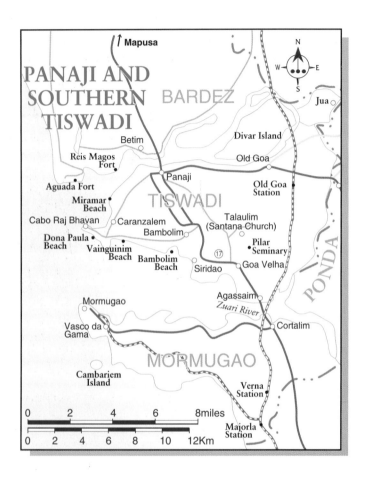

PANAJI AND SOUTHERN TISWADI

↑ Mapusa

N
W　E
S

BARDEZ

Jua

Betim

Divar Island

Reis Magos Fort

Old Goa

Aguada Fort

Panaji

Old Goa Station

Miramar Beach

TISWADI

Cabo Raj Bhavan

Caranzalem

Talaulim (Santana Church)

Bambolim

Dona Paula Beach

Pilar Seminary

Vainguinim Beach

Bambolim Beach

17

Siridao

Goa Velha

PONDA

Agassaim

Mormugao

Zuari River

Cortalim

Vasco da Gama

MORMUGAO

Cambariem Island

Verna Station

0　2　4　6　8miles
0　2　4　6　8　10　12Km

Majorla Station

Dona Paula Beach, just 7 km (4.33 miles) from Panaji, has a direct bus service to the capital. **The Dona Paula Beach Resort** is reasonably priced (no pool) but usually occupied by package tourists. To the east, the **Cidade de Goa**, one of Goa's largest (and most expensive) hotels, stretches along most of **Vainguirim Beach**, giving its patrons a sense of exclusivity. Built by Charles Correa, the hotel comprises low-rise blocks painted ochre and cream, reminiscent of a Greek 'cubist' village; its design won an architectural award. There are two splendid pools but as Vainguirim Beach faces the Zuari River estuary, the sea here is particularly calm and safe for bathing. Parachute gliding facilities are available

Dramatically sited near the point of Dona Paula's rocky headland is the modern *Image of India*, carved by the German sculptress Baroness Yrsa von Leistner. From the jetty below, the passenger ferry departs for the industrial town of **Mormugao**, below the headland on the opposite side of the bay. Remains of its fort overlook the port but there is little else of tourist interest.

The Pilar Seminary

From Panaji, a road winds south eastward for approximately 15 km (9.5 miles) to the Pilar Seminary, perched on a hilltop just north of Goa Velha.

Founded as a Capuchin convent in 1613, it was abandoned following the suppression of religious orders in 1835. Carmelites restored the buildings in 1858, but the seminary is now administered by the Missionary Society of St Francis Xavier, founded in 1940.

Access to the monastic church is via a splendid baroque entrance, built of stone. Immediately ahead is the tomb of **Agnelo d'Souza**, the seminary's spiritual director from 1918 until his death in 1927; d'Souza's canonization is confidently expected.

Within the church, traces of early frescoes survive right of the entrance. The high altar's reredos incorporates the painted figure of Our Lady of Pilar, which the Capuchins took with them when they left Spain in 1613; the angels at her feet are modern work. The building nearby was constructed recently for teaching purposes; it contains a chapel with an unusual, circular altar.

Further up the hill stands the original convent, with its two-storey cloisters. The complex occupies the site of a Kadamba temple dedicated to Govesvara, a locally popular form of Shiva. Damaged idols, including a headless Nandi bull, were discovered during excavations. These were formerly exhibited in the seminary's ground-floor museum (which may always be visited on request), but have recently been returned to the Hindu religious authorities; other ancient carvings of interest remain on display.

There are splendid views of the Goan countryside to be obtained from the seminary, including the convent's orchard and the water tank of the temple.

The old city of Gowapuri

Looking southward to the River Zuari estuary, it is now difficult to appreciate that a great port once lay at the foot of the hill, the deep waters of the Zuari flowing immediately past it. This was *Gowapuri* (later *Gova*), the city of the Kadamba kings, who made it their capital after departing from *Chandrapura* in 1052.

Gowapuri became India's major west coast port, the Bombay of its time, and remained the capital until 1312, when it was partly destroyed by the Sultan of Delhi's raiding troops: the Kadambas then returned, briefly, to *Chandrapura*.

The Bahmani Sultan conquered the city about 1350, imposing Islam on its inhabitants and destroying the Hindu temples. However, *Gowapuri* shortly fell to the Hindu Vijayanagars, in 1378,

Santana Church

The Church of St Anne, or Santana, as it is usually known, in Talaulim, is one of Goa's most splendid, in spite of the now unimportant status of its parish.

The façade was modelled on that of the great Augustinian church in Old Goa, of which only part of one tower has survived.

A legend that St Anne, mother of the Virgin Mary, had appeared to local villagers, led to the dedication of the first church on the site, which was built in the sixteenth century. This was replaced, in greatly enlarged form, in 1681-95, by the present building.

Neglected for many years, it is feared that Santana will eventually crumble away, like its village, restoration apparently being unaffordable.

The square flanking towers, in five stages, are only slightly recessed from the façade, and linked to it by three wide cornices, which give an impression of fortress-like strength. Simple pilasters reduce the severity of the towers, both of which are surmounted by balustrades, the line of the pilasters continuing through them and surmounted by pinnacles; further pinnacles punctuate each balustrade.

The three central bays of the façade are emphasized by pairs of Corinthian columns and a pedimented upper stage, linked by fan-shaped 'volutes' with the remainder; its recess accommodates a figure of St Anne.

Internally, the aisleless, white-painted nave is exceptionally high and light, the upper windows, which illuminate its vault, being an unusual feature in a Goan church. Arches along the sides of the nave support the galleries and are separated by simplified Corinthian pilasters.

Throughout the church, St Anne is depicted as a venerable lady, wearing a hat and holding a staff; by tradition, this was how she appeared to the parishoners of Talaulim.

who brutally slaughtered its Muslim inhabitants.

During their rule of a century, the river began to silt up and therefore *Gova* could no longer accommodate shipping. In 1470, the Bahmanis took the city once more and razed it to the ground; they then migrated to Ela, which was developing as a deepwater port.

Nothing remains of the great city, apart from the tank of its hillside temple, mentioned above. Throughout its three hundred years' existence, *Gowapuri* was also known as *Gopakpuri*, *Gopakkapattana* and, eventually, *Gova*. It is possible that all these names derived from Govesvara, the form in which Shiva is worshipped; if so, the god may also be ultimately responsible for Goa's name.

Goa Velha

A descent to Goa Velha village leads to the former centre of the great city, as indicated by a roadside board. Although there is nothing of much interest in the straggling village, from its square, during Holy Week, the unique **Procession of Saints** begins at the Church of St Andrew.

More than twenty figures of saints, sumptuously attired and mostly dating from the late nineteenth century, are paraded round the streets of Goa Velha on extravagantly decorated floats. The custom, begun by the Franciscans in the seventeenth century, was terminated in 1835, when religious orders were suppressed; it was revived in 1895.

Agassaim

Continuing south, the village of Agassaim is reached a short distance before the River Zuari bridge. To the left, rises its **Church of St Laurence**.

The unremarkable exterior of this eighteenth-century building is no preparation for the outstanding reredos to its high altar, which covers an entire wall. Such baroque extravagance is remarkable, even in Goa. Clusters of deeply carved and gilded pilasters, surmounted by candelabras, flank the halo'd figure of St Laurence. The restrained blue and white paintwork of the interior, particularly the chancel's coffered ceiling, admirably complements the exuberance of the piece.

Talaulim

The return journey may be interrupted, once Old Goa has been passed, by taking a detour, right, to the **Church of St Anne (Santana)** at Talaulim (not to be confused with Talauli in Sanguem *taluka*).

A good day to visit this great church is Sunday as then it is certain to be open; at other times it may be locked and the keys difficult to locate. It is regarded by many as the finest example of Goa's Indian baroque style to survive. The village, once thriving but now little more than a hamlet, was decimated by plague, due to its proximity to Old Goa.

A return to the main Panaji road is necessary, as the village's main road no longer continues to Old Goa.

3 Old Goa

Of the city itself, only a few vestiges of civic buildings, and no domestic, remain. What does still exist, however, is a cluster of great Renaissance and Baroque churches, dating from the sixteenth century, and now set amidst well-kept lawns, laid out where the streets and squares once stood. Old Goa's churches constitute the state's greatest architectural heritage. A visitor to Old Goa as early as 1827 was able to report, *'Nothing remains of the city but the sacred: the profane is entirely banished'*.

After transferring their capital to Panaji, the Portuguese referred to the city as *Velha Goa*, but this has now been anglicized to Old Goa, partly to avoid confusion with Goa Velha village.

Getting there

All tour operators include Old Goa on their itineraries, but there are regular bus services from Panaji, and privately-hired transport.

If a cursory visit is planned, then a coach tour will suffice. If, however, it is intended to spend some time in Old Goa and visit many of the buildings, a taxi or auto-rickshaw will be necessary.

The standard bus service will permit visitors to see the five most important buildings in their own time, as they are all within easy walking distance of each other: the Minor Basilica of Bom Jesus, the Se Cathedral, the Church of St Francis of Assisi, the Archaeological Museum and the Church of St Cajetan.

Admirably, no charge is levied for entering any areas in Old Goa. The churches are open daily from dawn to dusk, but the Archaeological Museum, which is open 10am to 5pm, closes on Fridays.

A Hindu Brahmin foundation

It is recorded that, in the thirteenth century, a colony of Brahmins was established on the site of Old Goa in a religious settlement, known as a Brahmapuri. A century later, two villages that had grown up nearby were combined to provide a further Brahmapuri.

Known as *Ela*, or *Ila*, with its deepwater harbour already developing as a port, the prospering village was adopted as their capital by the Bahmanis, after they had completely destroyed *Gowapuri* in

Opposite: A rare example of the Manueline style is the central doorway from 1521, re-used in the church of St Francis of Assisi's new building in 1661

1470. At some period, they also appear to have transferred the name *Gowapuri*, or *Gova*, to *Ela*.

Once again, however, their stay in Goa was brief, Yusuf Adil Shah, the first Sultan of Bijapur, occupying the city in 1488, and building his fortress palace there, the city's first structure of importance. It is known that, in addition to the palace, the walled Muslim city contained a moated fort and an important mosque.

Adil Shah's capital was Bijapur, and it has been surmised that the mosque, which he built there and still survives, would have resembled Gova's; it is high-domed but with modest minarets. Shortly before the Portuguese invasion, a traveller records that the city possessed several mosques and temples.

Portugese Conquest

In 1510, the Portuguese, under the leadership of Afonso de Albuquerque, finally took the city by defeating the forces of Yusuf's teenage son Ismail Adil Shah; thus began their 450-year occupancy of Goa.

Although the Muslims in *Gova* that had survived the battle were slaughtered, the Hindus were unharmed and permitted to remain. Albuquerque appropriated Adil Shah's palace, which became the Governor's residence, and, adjacent to it, he built Old Goa's first church. This was dedicated to St Catherine, to commemorate the taking of the city by the Portuguese on 25 November, St Catherine's Day.

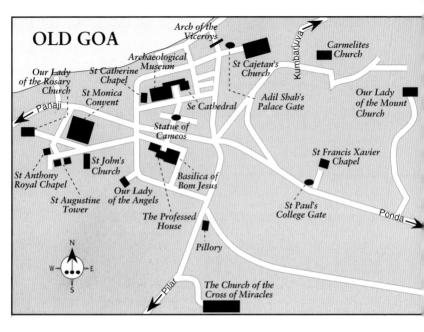

OLD GOA

Arch of the Viceroys
Carmelites Church
Archaeological Museum
St Cajetan's Church
Our Lady of the Rosary Church
St Catherine Chapel
Kumbarjua
Our Lady of the Mount Church
St Monica Convent
Panaji
Se Cathedral
Adil Shah's Palace Gate
Statue of Cameos
St Francis Xavier Chapel
St John's Church
Basilica of Bom Jesus
St Anthony Royal Chapel
Our Lady of the Angels
St Augustine Tower
St Paul's College Gate
Ponda
The Professed House
Pillory
Pilar
The Church of the Cross of Miracles

N W E S

Unlike the houses of Muslim *Ela*, which had been mostly single storey, those of the Portuguese city were two storey and interspersed with grand villas and palaces built in Portuguese colonial style.

In order to protect *Gova* against Muslim retaliation, the defensive wall was repaired and the fort remodelled in Portuguese style. The new conquerors simplified the name of their city to Goa, a name which would eventually incorporate all their Indian territories, including the enclaves north of Bombay.

Conversion to Christianity

Initially, the Portuguese believed that the Hindus were an exotic sect of Christians, but, on discovering that this was an error, Albuquerque instigated their conversion, which became the responsibility of the Franciscan friars that arrived in 1517.

Portuguese settlers were encouraged to intermarry with high-caste Goan ladies, but low-caste Hindus were attracted to Christianity in the belief, wrongly founded, that this new religion would break down caste differentials and thus better their lot. From the outset, Goans were regarded as Portuguese citizens rather than colonials.

Golden Goa

Throughout the sixteenth and the early seventeenth centuries, monasteries and great churches were built to accommodate thousands of worshippers. Goa became by far the most important colonial city in Asia, with a population exceeding a quarter of a million; greater than that of Lisbon itself.

Some travellers reported that

the city was even more splendid than Rome, and the renown of 'Golden Goa' was such that a mass exodus of immigrants from Portugal led to an excessive drain on the European power's labour force.

Unlike the houses of Muslim *Ela*, which had been mostly single storey, those of the Portugese city were two storey and interspersed with grand villas and palaces built in Portugese colonial style.

Plague and persecution

Disastrously, by the middle of the sixteenth century it had become obvious that the site for Goa's capital had been badly chosen.

Surrounded by pools of stagnant water left by the monsoons, it was ideal for the breeding of the anopheles mosquito and, in consequence, the spread of malaria. Also, the virtually non-existent drainage system which, bearing in mind the porous nature of the soil, led to the seepage of sewage into the drinking water wells, and resultant plagues; the eventual decimation of the population was inevitable.

In 1543, cholera struck for the first time and many citizens died. By the end of the seventeenth century, the population had dwindled from its peak of 200,000 to 20,000. Nevertheless, the building of churches and houses continued apace, and the city's southern boundaries almost reached Goa Velha.

Before the decline of the city, there had been more than fifty churches in Goa, many of which were monastic. The dreaded Inquisition arrived from Portugal in 1560 and its officials took over the vacant Viceroy's residence, remaining there until the abolition of the Inquisition in 1774. Trials of those accused of heresy, known as *autos-da-fé* (acts of faith), were held in the square outside.

Gradually, the River Mandovi silted up and, by the end of the seventeenth century, ships were having great difficulty in docking at Goa's port – the city was doomed.

In 1702, the viceroy, then residing at Panelim, a suburb of Old Goa, attempted to move the capital to Mormugao. The better-quality residences were stripped of building materials that could be re-used at the new site, and ordinary houses were left to fall into disrepair.

However, sufficient finance was not available for the scheme, and it was eventually abandoned in favour of a gradual move to Panaji. Although the great churches and convents remained standing, Portugal suppressed religious orders in 1835, and the city's monastic population departed: further ruination resulted.

Eight years later, the capital was officially transferred to Panaji, where the viceroys had been in residence since 1759.

The architecture of Old Goa

As the conversion of Goans to Christianity was the responsibility of European-based monastic

Goan stone

A great misfortune for Goa was that the local stone, laterite, although easy to carve, weathered extremely badly, and had to be given a protective coating of plaster covered with a lime wash. It was necessary to renew the latter annually after each monsoon, otherwise the black fungus which formed on the damp surfaces would rot the plaster, thus exposing the laterite.

When this relatively expensive procedure was neglected, the red laterite would simply fade away, as dramatically demonstrated on the east façade of Bom Jesus at Old Goa. For some detailing, such as decorative columns and architraves, basalt was brought in from other Indian states; the west façade of Bom Jesus is one of the finest examples of the contrast between red laterite and grey basalt, which creates an attractive polychrome effect.

orders, it is hardly surprising that the design of Goa's churches, and their embellishments, should follow contemporary European styles. Most were built when late-Renaissance was giving way to baroque, particularly in Italy, which provided the inspiration for many Portuguese architects.

However, a few of Goa's earliest churches followed the idiosyncratic Portuguese style known as Manueline, after King Manuel I (1495-1521), in which much use was made of naturalistic decorative themes, many of them appertaining to the sea, such as ropes and anchors. Unfortunately, most Manueline churches have been rebuilt, and only Our Lady of the Rosary, and the doorway of St Francis of Assisi, both in Old Goa, remain as examples of that style.

While all the architects involved were European, mostly Portuguese but some Italian, the actual construction of the buildings was the responsibility of local craftsmen, who did their best to follow the detailed but unfamiliar instructions with which they were provided. Some of the results approach contemporary European standards, but many find the cruder examples equally endearing.

Virtually all the state's church interiors are baroque in style, and feature gilded altarpieces. Paintings on wood are by local artists, many of them aided by Italians, while the few that are on canvas were painted in Europe and imported. As may be expected, most carved figures are of wood, but a few imports of stone do exist.

The Minor Basilica of Bom Jesus

Goa's most important building, the Minor Basilica of Bom Jesus, contains the remains of St Francis Xavier.

Bom Jesus: Old Goa's most impressive church façade

Bom Jesus (Good Jesus) was built for worship by the members of the Convent of Jesuits. Their 'professed house', where they lived and worked, had been completed in 1589, but its church was not begun until 1594; consecration took place in 1605. Pope Pius XII elevated the church to Minor Basilica status in 1964.

The exterior

Uniquely among Goa's churches, the original lime-washed plaster has been purposely removed from most of its surface, and the soft red laterite exposed. The riskiness of this experiment is immediately apparent, as some of the detailing, particularly at the rear of the building, has already faded.

The most important feature of the exterior of Bom Jesus is its west façade, more sumptuously decorated than that of any other Goan church. Features are carved in basalt stone, while here the laterite has always been left exposed to contrast with it. As is usual in Renaissance churches, the Ionic, Doric and Corinthian Orders appear in ascending order.

Circular windows and fan-shaped volutes at the upper level are, however, baroque features. As they rise in succession, the first three stages decrease in height, but, conversely, their decoration increases in richness.

Surprisingly, the pedimented gable provides the deepest stage, giving a rather top-heavy appearance to the church. It bears the inscription IHS, the first three letters that spell Jesus in Greek.

Major attractions of Old Goa

It should be noted that Old Goa can be approached from several directions. On arrival, however, most visitors proceed directly to the **Basilica of Bom Jesus**, continuing northward to the **Se Cathedral**, the **Church of St Francis of Assisi** and the **Archaeological Museum**, which together form one group. Immediately to the east lies the **Church of St Cajetan**. This tour proves sufficient for most, but enthusiasts may continue westward and eastward to explore further churches.

This is a mandatory feature of Jesuit churches, appearing amidst the heads and wings of angels, and here surmounted by the royal crown and a cross.

It is believed that the façade was modelled on Old Goa's Church of St Paul, now lost; like that building, and, unusual for an important church in Goa, there are no flanking towers.

A free-standing bell tower, south of the apse, at the east end, is Italianate in style and unique of its type in Goa. Also unique is the cruciform plan of the building, with its protruding transepts. Flying buttresses on the north side are not original features, but were added comparitively recently to strengthen the structure.

The interior

On entering the church, immediately left, an exuberantly carved wooden figure of St Francis Xavier stands between twisted columns.

Two columns at the west end of the nave support the choir gallery above. Inscriptions in Portuguese and Latin fixed to them record that the building of the church began on 24 November 1594, and that Aleixo de Menezes, Archbishop of Goa and Primate of India, consecrated Bom Jesus 15 May 1605.

The interior of the church is much plainer than the façade would indicate, only the baroque, gilded altarpieces providing richness. The wooden ceiling is modern work, but the galleries are original; visitors of consequence sat there throughout important services.

Dom Jeronimo Mascarenhas, Captain of Cochin, left sufficient money in his will for the church to be built. He died in 1593, and his memorial stands against the north wall, half-way up the nave. Opposite this, against the south wall, is the outstanding canopied pulpit, sumptuously carved.

The high altar's reredos, covered in gold leaf, incorporates figures of the infant Jesus and St Ignatius Loyola, founder of the Jesuit order.

The north transept accommodates the chapel of the Blessed Sacrament, and the south transept the chapel of St Francis Xavier.

The Sacristy

The east passageway leads from the high altar, past the chapel

St Francis Xavier

St Francis Xavier, Portugal's most influential Christian missionary to Asia, died on his return journey to Goa from Japan in 1552, aged 46, and his body, like that of Christopher Columbus, has found many resting places.

The body of the saint was first buried where he died, on Sancian Island off the coast of southern China, but it was soon transferred to Malacca, before being reburied in Old Goa's Church of St Paul in 1554. While in Goa, St Francis had resided at the College of St Paul. On completion of the Jesuits' Professed House, his remains were moved to it, but transferred yet again, to this church, in 1624.

of St Francis Xavier, to an exceptional doorway, the entrance to the sacristy (open, except Fridays, 09.00 to 12.30 and 14.00 to 17.30). This doorway, the finest in Goa, comprises a sculpted stone surround, again bearing the IHS monogram of Christ, and a door of carved wooden panels. An unsympathetic striplight, recently fixed to the lintel, is not an original feature!

Within, the room has a coffered vault and a south apse, which accommodates the altar. Carved

The Tomb of St Francis Xavier

The south transept of the Basilica of Bom Jesus was converted to form St Francis Xavier's mausoleum in 1655, a passageway being added to two of its sides. Paintings and carvings depict scenes from the life of the saint.

The centrally positioned tomb, Goa's most venerated shrine, was the gift of one of the later members of the Italian Medici family, Cosimo III, Grand Duke of Tuscany, who presented it in return for the pillow on which the saint's head rested following his death.

The Florentine, Giovanni Batista Foggini, designed the piece, a task which took him ten years. Sections were prepared in Italy and shipped to Goa in 1698. The jasper base of the tomb incorporates marble carvings.

Above this, a grey jasper stage displays four bronze plaques, which depict missionary activities of St Francis, including his desperate swim to escape from natives on the island of Morro, who apparently did not appreciate the saint's attempts to save their souls. These bronzes are the finest European works of art to be found in Goa.

The solid silver casket in which the saint lies was not part of the Italian gift; it is Goan work, made in 1636. Precious stones originally studded the piece, but all have been lost.

Renowned for their good state of preservation, the remains of St Francis Xavier are displayed to the congregation of Bom Jesus, at approximately ten yearly intervals, on 3 December, the anniversary of his death. However, parts of the saint's mortal remains no longer lie within the reliquary, mainly due to the high regard in which relics were held in former times.

An acquisitive lady venerator bit off a toe, holding it in her mouth as she left the church, and her descendants still retain this macabre relic in Lisbon. A section of an arm was removed in 1615 and despatched to the church of Il Gesu in Rome, the mother church of the Jesuits. In 1619, part of the right hand was sent to Japan.

chests, containing clerical vestments, line the walls, on which paintings of saints are displayed.

Pope Pius XII presented Goa with a rose cast in gold in 1953 and this is kept in an iron chest beneath the altar.

A nineteenth-century painting depicts the exceptional state of preservation of St Xavier's remains at that time. Within a glass case may be seen one of the saint's toes, which became detached from his corpse in 1890. Buried in front of the altar is the founder of the sacristy, Balthazar de Veiga, who died in 1659.

In the exhibition room above the sacristy a small display includes scenes painted from the life of St Francis by a modern artist. From this room there is a good view of the saint's tomb below.

Top: *The façade of Old Goa's cathedral*

Above: *The rear of Bom Jesus demonstrates how badly laterite, the local stone, wears if unprotected by plaster and paint*

From Bom Jesus to the Se Cathedral

On leaving the church, note the rather grim façade of the Jesuits' monastic quarters attached to its west end and known as the **Professed House**. Constructed in 1585-9, a fire destroyed much of it in 1633, and not all was rebuilt. A number of Jesuit fathers still maintain a teaching establishment here.

In the centre of the short road linking Bom Jesus and the cathedral is the **Statue of Camões** (1960), Portugal's national poet, who wrote in the sixteenth century. He is depicted holding the scroll on which is written his epic poem *The Lusiads*, composed in Goa, which records Vasco da Gama's voyage to India. The sculptor does not neglect to demonstrate that Camões had lost the use of one eye.

Immediately ahead stands Old Goa's largest surviving group of buildings; from right to left: The Se Cathedral, the Church of St Francis of Assisi, the Archaeological Museum (behind the church), and the small, free-standing Chapel of St Catherine.

Se Cathedral

The Se Cathedral is the largest of Old Goa's structures, and the Portuguese government intended, from its conception, that this would be the most important of their colonial churches in Asia. It remains the most extensive building in Goa and the largest church in Asia. Begun in 1562 on the site of a mosque, progress was slow, and the interior was not completed until 1652.

The cathedral was paid for by selling the possessions of Goan Hindus who had died intestate. A Hindu was considered intestate if he had not converted to Christanity and his marriage been solemnized in a church!

Exterior

Although built expressly for the Dominican order, like so many

Chapel of St Catherine

The Chapel of St Catherine, a small, free-standing structure at the west end of the cathedral complex, commemorates the first church to be built in Goa by the Portuguese.

Erected by Albuquerque shortly after he reconquered the city on 25 November 1510, it is believed to have been hastily formed of mud and straw but, two years later, was superseded by a more solid structure, presumably of laterite stone.

Although always small, St Catherine's was granted cathedral status by Paul III's papal bull of 1534, and it retained this until the present cathedral was consecrated; no other parish church existed in Goa until 1542. The building was enlarged in 1550 by Governor George Cabral, and shortly afterwards, through a further papal bull, St Catherine's became the

Goan churches of its period the design was greatly influenced by Jesuit architecture. Nevertheless, the Manueline tradition of square, flanking towers to the main façade was maintained.

Unusually, the cathedral faces east rather than west. The north tower was lost in 1776 after being struck by lightning; the south tower accommodates what is

archiepiscopal metropolitan church of India.

On the enlarged structure, a plaque recorded that Albuquerque's troops had entered Old Goa 'in this place', implying that the gateway in the Moslem city's wall had been located here.

Shortly before their expulsion from Goa, the Portuguese rebuilt St Catherine's, and some of the original work was replicated; much of the façade may have been retained. Typical Goan flanking towers linked to the pediments by volutes appear to have influenced the design of the present cathedral. Internally, with only one altarpiece, all is very plain.

On the way to the Church of St Cajetan, which lies north-east of the cathedral, are passed Old Goa's only remnants of buildings not directly appertaining to the Roman Catholic church.

known as the 'Golden Bell', due to its resonant tone.

Interior

The cathedral, entered from its east façade, is aisled, and chapels on both the north and south sides are separated by internal buttresses. Both columns supporting the choir incorporate holy water stoups decorated with figures of St Francis Xavier and St Ignatius Loyola.

Transferred here from Albuquerque's small church of St Catherine, which served as Goa's first cathedral, is the **baptismal font**, accommodated in the north chapel. An inscription records that Jorge Gomez presented this in 1532. It is alleged that St Francis Xavier baptized converts from the font.

The third chapel on the north side is dedicated to **The Cross of Miracles** (referred to in a Goan legend), and its carved wooden screen is exceptional. At the west end of the cathedral, the reredos to the high altar is deeply carved with scenes from the life and martyrdom of St Catherine, to whom the building is dedicated. An eighteenth-century organ is housed in the gallery. From the north-west corner, a door leads to the barrel-vaulted sacristy; its altar incorporates a model of St Peter's Cathedral in Rome.

Church of St Francis of Assisi

To enter the Church of St Francis of Assisi, walk westward from the cathedral. This was the church of the convent, similarly dedicated to St Francis, the domestic buildings of which lay immediately behind, linked with the cathedral by the former Archbishop's Palace.

The present church, constructed in 1661, replaced an earlier building of 1521 dedicated to the Holy Ghost. This had originated as a small chapel erected soon after the arrival in Goa of the Franciscans in 1517.

Exterior

Both towers that flank the façade are octagonal, rather than square as is usual. The Manueline doorway, re-used from the previous building, is Goa's only architectural feature of note in this style to have survived. Baroque exuberance at the upper level provides a strong contrast with the Classical severity of the adjacent cathedral. Its central niche accommodates a statue of St Michael.

Interior

Although no longer used for services, the interior of the church is one of Goa's most impressive baroque examples, with much intricate carving and delightful floral decoration to the walls and coffered ceiling.

Against the north wall, the pulpit is one of Goa's finest; its intricate carving of flora exhibits Indian taste. Boldly-sculpted tombstones form the pavement of the nave. Paintings of scenes from the life of St Francis line the chancel walls, those on the north side being in much better condition.

The high altar's reredos is gilded and covers the entire east wall. Its pedimented top section depicts St Francis on a pedestal inscribed with his vows: poverty, humility and obedience. From his crucifix, Christ embraces the saint with one arm.

Archaeological Museum

The Archaeological Museum occupies the former domestic section of the Franciscan monastery, and is entered immediately left of the church. Rebuilding of the cloister in 1707 and additional construction work in 1765 has meant that the buildings that accommodate the museum now form, in essence, an eighteenth-century replacement of the sixteenth-century original.

The museum was founded in 1964, but exhibits were rearranged in 1983 to take advantage of increased space made available; it is open 10am-5pm, but closed Fridays.

A sixteenth-century, contemporary bronze statue of the Portuguese conqueror of Goa, Afonso de Albuquerque, stands in the vestibule. Initially, this was located just within the entrance gate to Old Goa but was moved to more prominent positions as the city grew. It was transferred to the centre of Panaji in 1847, and later to the Miramar quarter of Panaji, overlooking the beach, from where it was returned to Old Goa, and its present site.

Ahead lies the Key Gallery, subdivided by a display case into Goa's pre-Portuguese and

Portuguese history.

The most important exhibit is the centrally positioned Hindu carving of Vishnu, believed to be approximately one thousand years old. Flanking Vishnu are his consort, Laxmi, and the winged Garuda; the ten *avatars* (incarnations) of Vishnu are each depicted within the carved surround to its head. From bottom left clockwise (not in chronological order): Matsya, the fish; Varaha, the boar; Yamana, the dwarf; Parashurama; Kalki; Buddha; Rama; Krishna; Narasimha, the man/lion and Kurma, the tortoise.

Other Hindu figures of note in this gallery include the goddess Mahish Mardini decapitating a demon (eleventh century); Laxmi anointed with water by elephants and Shiva embracing his consort. Stones carved to depict heroic deaths, and *sati* (a widow's ritual suicide) are also displayed.

The Portuguese Occupation section consists mainly of religious carvings and portraits in oils; its **Portrait Gallery** is approached from the stairs and occupies the upper floor of the cloisters. Most portraits are of the sixty viceroys or governors who ruled Goa in the name of the Portuguese Crown for four hundred and fifty years.

Dom Joao de Castro sat for the first portrait in 1547, and commissioned representations of his twelve predeccesors to be painted at the same time. Among these was the explorer Vasco da Gama, who was governor for three months until his death, at Goa, in 1524.

Most of the paintings, which are displayed chronologically, have been heavily restored, Goa's monsoon not being conducive to the preservation of oil paint. Restoration was not of the highest standard, and the chief interest of the collection to visitors is its record of Goan court dress.

The last painting displayed is a portrait of the dictator Salazar, president of Portugal at the time of India's takeover of Goa in 1961. The portraits that predate the present century are painted on wood. All were originally housed in the governors' various residences before being brought here from the Secretariat in 1962.

The **Sculpture Gallery** is accommodated in the open courtyard of the cloister. In the centre is the figure of St Catherine, which stood on Old Goa's original Arch of the Viceroys, but was ommitted when this was rebuilt.

Those interested in 'relics' will note, left of the entrance, a stone pillar from the hill near Madras, where, by tradition, St Thomas was martyred; this incorporates what is alleged to be a section of the lance that killed the apostle. The pillar, set in a glass-fronted recess, forms a shrine, which was constructed in 1630.

Most other sculptures displayed are Hindu hero and *sati* stones. In adjoining rooms are models of a seventeenth-century Portuguese caravel (minus rigging) and the fortress of Diu, formerly part of Goa, although situated north of Bombay.

The Arch of the Viceroys

From the east façade of the cathedral, the second road left is straddled by the Arch of the Viceroys. Vasco da Gama's grandson, Francisco da Gama, was appointed Governor of Goa in 1597, and, two years later, built a ceremonial entrance in the city wall from the river. This collapsed in 1948 but was rebuilt in 1954.

Ahead, the south face of the archway, built of undecorated laterite, is its least important. The crowned figure of a female standing on a turbaned, prostrate man, appears to represent Christianity overcoming Hinduism. Within the arch, a plaque dated 1599 records the erection of the earlier structure. A further inscription commemorates Dom João IV, the first king to rule Portugal following its emancipation from Spain in 1640.

The river side of the arch is far more splendid, its laterite being faced with granite. Within a niche stands the figure of **Vasco da Gama**, a modern replacement of the original. The deer frieze of the arch had been Vasco da Gama's crest. It is unlikely that this side of the arch bears much resemblance to its predecessor, as that incorporated a further stage, in which stood the bronze statue of St Catherine, now displayed in the Archaeological Museum.

Fragments of the city wall can be seen near the arch, but nothing survives of the Customs House, which once stood between the arch and the river.

From the river, passing through the arch, stretched Old Goa's main street, Rua Direita (Straight Street). It is now hard to comprehend that this was once lined with shops selling exotic goods, and led to the city's most important square. On the left stood the palace of Adil Shah.

The Gateway of the Palace of Adil Shah

A road, left, leads to the Church of St Cajetan; in front of its west façade stands the Gateway of the Palace of Adil Shah, the only surviving relic of the old palace.

After the governors of Goa transferred their residence to the suburb of Panelim in 1754, the great two-storey palace, built by Yusuf Adil Shah in 1488, fell into disrepair. In 1820, it was carefully demolished and re-useable building material transferred to Panaji.

The basalt section of the former entranceway is all that survives of the palace; it consists of a lintel supported by carved pillars. Decoration of the pillars is Brahmin in style and they are, therefore, believed to have been taken from a Hindu shrine and re-used here by the Moslems.

Fragments of screens beside the columns are similarly reminiscent of examples in Hindu temples. The lintel bears scrollwork which is obviously Portuguese, and must have been added when the palace was remodelled for the governors.

Church of St Cajetan

The Church of St Cajetan was built 1656-61 by friars of the Italian Theatine Order, founded by St Cajetan, who lived in Goa for a short period.

The design of the west façade is based on that originally prepared by Carlo Maderna for St Peter's Rome, but the side bays are omitted which link that building to Bernini's colonnades, and there are bell turrets at the corners instead of the cupolas of St Peter's. In 1993, after some years of neglect, the exterior was painted cream, and partly restored.

Rounded Corinthian pilasters, support the central, the others being flat. The theme of alternatives is continued by the architraves: triangular above the side doors and curved above the niches, in which stand figures of the Evangelists. As at St Peter's, windows at the third stage are balustraded.

This is the only surviving domed church in Goa, and another similarity with St Peter's is that the dome is obscured from view at close quarters by the height of the façade. A drum supports the dome, which is surmounted by a lantern. As has already been noted, a few other churches in Goa appear to be domed, but their 'domes' are imitations, purely serving as an external embellishment.

Within, the church is Greek Cross in plan, four great piers supporting the dome. Directly beneath is a well which, it has been suggested, may be a remnant from a Hindu temple that once existed on the site. The seven altarpieces are richly gilded. From the south-east pier projects a carved wooden pulpit.

The high altar is dedicated to Our Lady of the Divine Providence, the original dedication of the church. Its reredos is the only free-standing example in Goa. Beneath lies a small crypt, where the embalmed bodies of Goan governors were laid in lead caskets prior to their return to Portugal for burial. It appears that three were never transported, as their caskets remain.

Holy Hill

Most visitors will now have completed their tour of the churches of Old Goa, but several less important specimens remain for the enthusiast. West of Bom Jesus lies another complex of buildings sited on raised ground known as Holy Hill.

The first building seen, at the fork in the road, is the **Convent and Church of St John of God**. Begun in 1685, this was abandoned in 1835, and eventually purchased by the nearby Convent of St Monica as a residential home. Immediately preceeding their expulsion from Goa, the Portuguese restored the convent, completely replacing its roof.

Convent of St Monica

On the slope of the hill, facing the church of St John of God, the Convent of St Monica is one of the largest structures in Goa. The first buildings, constructed in 1606-27, were almost completely destroyed by fire in 1636, but rebuilding began the following year. At that time, St Monica's was the only convent in Goa to accommodate nuns.

The square complex is laid out around a large sunken courtyard incorporating a formal garden. Its four cloisters were originally vaulted, but now have timber ceilings. Great buttresses support the structure, both externally and from within the courtyard. In 1964, the Mater Dei Institute was founded here to encourage the study of theology by nuns, whatever their Order.

The church may be entered by pushing the bell. Most of the original murals have been whitewashed over, but faded traces survive on the west wall. Against the north wall, the pulpit is a splendid example, intricately carved. Opposite, the altarpiece is in similar style. The high altar's reredos, standing in a deep, apse-like niche, incorporates a figure of St Monica.

The Tower of St Augustine

To the south of St Monica, still dominating Holy Hill, is the Tower of St Augustine, the survivor of one of the twin towers of the St Augustine Monastery's church.

This fragment retains the complete tower's original height of 46m (150ft), and hints at the impressiveness of the original five-storey façade. Formerly, towers flanked both sides of the church, as is usual in Goa. Apparently, the Church of Santana at Talaulim, which still exists to the south of Old Goa, was modelled on St Augustine's.

The monastery had been founded by the Augustinians on their arrival at Goa in 1572, and was twice rebuilt in extended

The Royal Chapel of St Anthony

West of the Tower of St Augustine on Holy Hill, is the Royal Chapel of St Anthony.

Commissioned and dedicated by Albuquerque to the national saint of Portugal, the original chapel was built in 1534, but completely reconstructed shortly before the Portuguese left Goa in 1961.

As St Anthony is the patron saint of the Portuguese army, his statue was formally given the rank of captain and taken in procession each year to the Treasury to receive a captain's salary.

Allegedly, two governors decided to terminate this ceremony, but both were seriously injured in falls on St Anthony's feast day. Not surprisingly, they subsequently abandoned their plans!

The design of the church is unusual in that it is entered from a curved apse.

Above: Old Goa's Church of St Cajetan, completed in 1661, echoes the original design for the façade of St Peter's in Rome

Right: Detail from the pillars of a doorway – all that remains of Adil Shah's great Palace in Old Goa. The doorway was probably reused from a Hindu Temple

form. The monks added the Church of Our Lady of Grace in 1602, but all was abandoned in 1835 following the suppression of religious orders, and the monastery was demolished in 1846.

The shell of the church survived, but gradually became ruinous; by 1931, only its façade and one tower remained but, later that year, the façade collapsed completely, taking one side of the tower with it. The bell, Goa's second largest, was removed from the belfry and transferred to the Church of Our Lady of the Immaculate Conception in Panaji, where it remains.

The Church of Our Lady of The Rosary

Continue to the western extremity of Holy Hill, where the ground falls away steeply, to the Church of Our Lady of The Rosary.

A plaque records that from here, on 25 November 1510, Albuquerque watched the progress of the battle that was to be decisive in Portugal's conquest of Goa. He vowed to build a church on the site, and a simple structure was erected soon after his victory.

St Francis Xavier preached within that building in 1542, shortly after his arrival in Goa. He is also likely to have preached in the present church, which was consecrated in 1549. It is the oldest complete structure to survive in Old Goa, and the only one that St Francis could have seen.

Externally, high-sited windows and rounded towers are rare Goan examples of the Manueline style. However, decorative Manueline details are restricted to the twisted ropework carved on the bell tower at the west end.

As the church is open only on special occasions, few visitors are able to view the simple but delightful interior, with its beamed roof. The reredos of the high altar is refreshingly undemonstrative, in contrast with the huge, gilded baroque pieces seen elsewhere in Goa.

Caterina a Piro was the first Portuguese woman to arrive in Goa, and her marble tomb stands within the chancel. This is one of the earliest works in Goa to combine Classical European and Hindu (Gujerat) motifs. In front of the chancel is the tomb of her husband, Governor Garcia de Sa, who is commemorated by a simple slab. It is alleged that their marriage was sanctified by St Francis Xavier himself — but only when Caterina was on her deathbed.

Returning eastward, a right turn leads past Our Lady of the Angels (a church of scant interest) and continues ahead following the south side of the Bom Jesus basilica.

The Pillory

The next right turn leads southward to Old Goa's former pillory, now standing at the intersection of two roads. Originally, this marked the centre of the city's most important market square.

The pillory is in the form of two superimposed basalt

columns, linked by iron brackets and erected on a stepped pedestal. The columns, believed to have been taken from the Saptakoteshwar temple on Jua Island, were formerly provided with iron rings to which miscreants were tied; they were then publicly tortured, whipped and left in ignominy. The pillory fell into disuse in the early eighteenth century.

Few will wish to proceed further south to the ruined convent **Church of the Cross of Miracles**, founded in 1619 and rebuilt in 1674. The cross referred to in the dedication was transferred from this church to the cathedral in 1845.

The Archway of the Church of the College of St Paul

Return to the roundabout and follow the eastbound road (fourth left), which serves as the main road to Ponda. After approximately 120 metres, the Archway of the Church of the College of St Paul is seen on the north side.

This arch originally formed the main entrance to the church of the College of St Paul, and is all that survives of the building, which was consecrated on 25 January 1543 to commemorate St Paul's conversion. It allegedly occupies the site of a Hindu temple.

The secular buildings of the college had been completed a year earlier. Here, converts to Christianity were trained to become preachers, and, to assist them, a Konkani grammar was begun, the first to formalize in writing a modern Indian language. An epidemic in 1570 led to the abandonment of most of the college, and its dilapidated remnants were transported to Panaji for use as building material in 1832.

The Chapel of St Francis Xavier

A short road leads northward to the Chapel of St Francis Xavier.

St Francis lodged at the College of St Paul during most of his time in Goa, spending his nights at prayer in a small chapel; it was in this chapel that his remains were first laid when they were brought to Goa from Malacca in 1554. The chapel is known to have been in existence in 1545, and was originally dedicated to St Anthony (or possibly St Jerome), but, on his canonization, in 1662, it was re-dedicated to St Francis.

Like the remainder of the complex, the chapel fell into disrepair, and was completely rebuilt in 1884.

The Church of Our Lady of the Mount

The easiest way for motorists to reach the Church of Our Lady of the Mount is via the road to Cumbarjua. Return from the St Paul's Archway to the roundabout and take the fourth road right. The second turning right, at the Palm Grove bar, leads eastward, and a junction ahead is marked by a cross; the right fork should be taken. Vehicles will now have to be parked, but the tree-lined walk to the church is short and pleasant.

An alternative route, for those with a motorbike or prepared to undertake a lengthy trek once they have had to park, is to continue on the Ponda road approximately 100 metres east of the Archway of the Church of St Paul. A path, indicated by a painted cross, meanders northward. After taking the first left fork, the church may be seen on its hill rising above the trees. The last part of the journey, which must be walked, terminates in a long flight of steps.

Although this church can hardly be called one of the architectural jewels of Old Goa, from its steps are gained fine views of the surrounding great churches, and the leafy remoteness of the building creates a sense of personal discovery.

It may initially appear that nature is taking over, but the building itself is not ruinous and, in recent years, a huge tree, the roots of which threatened the structure, was removed. From the steps, looking westward, are seen, from left to right: the ruined tower of St Augustine, the Church of Our Lady of the Rosary (both on Holy Hill), the Church of St Francis of Assisi, the cathedral, which adjoins it, and the domed Church of St Cajetan.

A plaque on the side wall at the west end of Our Lady of the Mount records that Adil Shah's troops gathered on this hill in May 1510, before retaking Goa from Albuquerque, and again, in November that year, prior to their unsuccessful defence of the city.

Albuquerque commissioned Our Lady of the Mount as part of his votive offering for victory, and its existence is first recorded in 1519. The original church was probably very small, and appears to have been enlarged twice; however, it is possible that the fabric of the early building remains in part. Unfortunately, local graffiti 'artists' have taken advantage of the remoteness of the building, and it is hard to ignore their vandalism.

A door at the east end of the north wall generally gives access to the building. The nave has lost most of its decoration, and the pulpit has gone, but the reredoses of the high altar, dedicated to Our Lady, and the side altars, dedicated respectively to St Anthony and St Andrew, have survived. A memorial slab facing the high altar, inscribed with a skull and crossbones, marks the tomb of Antonio Alvares Pereira, the Portuguese architect of the first church.

The Church of the Carmelites

The last of Old Goa's buildings, the Church of the Carmelites, is seen by continuing northward on the road to Cumbarjua. However, only its façade remains and once more it is sited on a hilltop. The church was built in 1621, but the Carmelites refused to swear allegiance to the King of Portugal and were expelled from Goa in 1707.

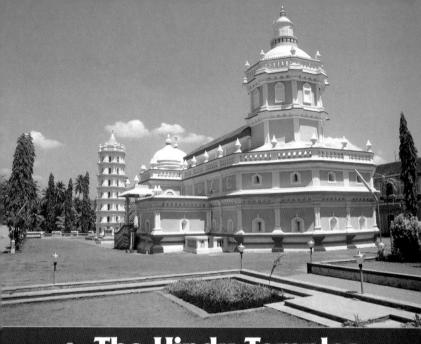

4 The Hindu Temples of Ponda

Easily reached from Panaji or Old Goa, Ponda's temples will provide visitors with a refreshing architectural contrast, and a reminder that they really are in India rather than a tropicalized Algarve. A morning spent viewing Old Goa's churches, followed by afternoon visits to some of Ponda's Hindu temples, makes a convenient, if rather full, day trip.

The rapidly expanding town of **Ponda** itself is of no particular interest, apart from some lively shops and a ruined fort, which encompasses the *dargah* (shrine) of a Muslim saint.

From 1540, all the temples in the Old Conquests (approx-imately 550) and the mosques were systematically demolished by order of the Viceroy, as part of the Portuguese attempt to convert the local population to Christianity. The *taluka* of Ponda did not finally come under Portuguese control until 1764, by

Above: *The Shri Mangesh Temple at Priol*

which time the excesses of the Inquisition were at an end, and religious freedom tacitly permitted throughout Goa.

Many Hindus living under Portuguese rule in the Old Conquests had refused to convert to Christianity, and, before their temples were destroyed, relocated idols and other treasures to the adjoining *taluka* of Ponda, where they would be relatively, although not entirely, safe from destruction. The idols were either transferred to existing temples or temporary refuges in the wooded valleys. Not only, therefore, is the oldest-established and most concentrated group of temples in Goa to be found in Ponda, but also the most ancient Hindu idols.

Getting there

As the vast majority of tourists stay in the coastal *taluka*s of Bardez, Tiswadi, Mormugao or Salcete, all of which the Portuguese had acquired by 1543 to form the Old Conquests, they will see few buildings of interest that are not European in style unless an excursion to another *taluka* is made.

Ponda *taluka* is separated from Tiswadi *taluka* by the Cumbarjua waterway, which is crossed by the long-established **Banastari Bridge**, lying just 5 km (3 miles) east of Old Goa: this is the easiest approach for visitors staying at the northern beach resorts.

For those staying at the southern beaches, Ponda is more conveniently reached via the bridge across the River Zuari at **Borim**.

The importance of hiring a driver who knows the *exact* locations of all the following temples cannot be stressed too greatly. Often, it will prove safer to change vehicles at Ponda, as few drivers from other areas are familiar with Ponda's temples apart from Shri Mangesh.

Shri Mangesh Temple

Although not particularly large, the first temple reached, after crossing the bridge at Banastari and following the road southward towards the town of Ponda, is the Shri Mangesh Temple of **Priol**, Goa's most famous, and frequently the only temple that tourists will be taken to see.

Note that it is a very long distance from Priol village, its name referring to the Priol administrative district.

History

Mangesh, an aspect of Shiva, is unique to Goa. The temple of Priol was built to house the god's *lingam*, which had previously been worshipped in the ancient Mangesh temple at *Kushastali* (now Cortalim), on the south bank of the River Zuari. This was transported by ferry to its present site shortly before the temple was demolished. On arrival in Ponda, the *lingam* was hidden amidst trees.

The Portuguese were known to make illegal forays into *taluka*s that adjoined the Old Conquests if they knew that 'their' idols had been transferred clandestinely to them; discretion, therefore, was essential. Hindus living in the Old Conquests were forbidden to cross the border to worship in the temples, but many did so as there was little difficulty in crossing the narrow Cumbarjua waterway; however, they risked heavy punishment, sometimes even death, if caught by marauding Portuguese officials.

In the mid-eighteenth century, the ruling Raja of Sunda donated land, the income from which was used to build and maintain the temple.

A few years later, when the administration of Ponda was transferred to the Portuguese, part of the agreement was that there would be no interference with the temple or its endowment, and the estate still exists, operated by descendants of the original trustees. Not only has this ensured regular maintenance, it has also permitted extensions to be made to the temple.

Exterior

Before entering the complex, follow the long path descending to the great water tank, one of the largest in a Goan temple, and probably the oldest element at Priol to survive unaltered; it may date from the eighteenth century.

Corner gateways lead to the temple's courtyard, which is dominated by the seven-stage lamp tower, painted gleaming white. The domes of the temple itself

are also white, but blue and yellow enliven much of the exterior.

Around the courtyard, buildings accommodate offices, workshops, reception rooms, and living quarters for pilgrims (*agarshalas*). Right of the main entrance to the temple is the *vrindavan* (giant flower pot), colourfully decorated with tiles. Pilasters, balustrades and a lantern above the main dome are all European baroque features. A palanquin (*palki*) stands in one of the aisles; this serves as a sedan chair when the temple's main idol is transported short distances.

Interior

Within the temple, non-Hindus will be surprised by the animation of the worshippers; half-naked children shriek and play, women gossip and men discuss business; very unlike the hushed atmosphere of a Christian church or a Muslim mosque. All eyes are drawn to the silver-clad screen of the sanctuary at the far end of the *mandapam*. Shiva's bull, Nandi, guards the shrine, which is flanked by the elephant-headed Ganesh, and Bhagavati, a manifestation of Shiva's consort.

Shri Mahalsa Temple

By continuing southward for 1 km (two thirds of a mile) on the main road to Ponda, and turning right at the approach to **Mardol** village, the Shri Mahalsa Temple, the next important temple, is reached.

The history of this temple is similar to that of Priol: its god was

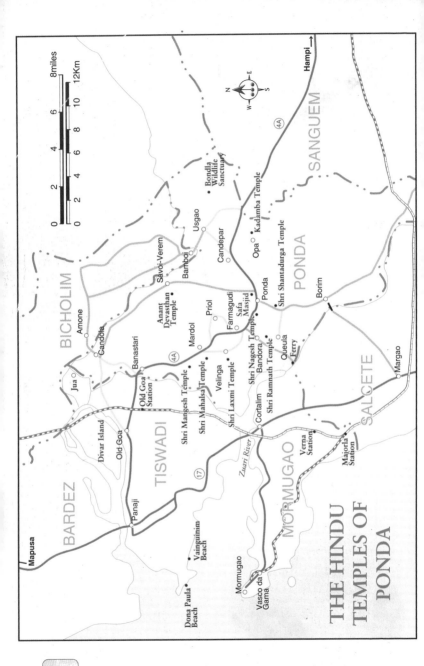

THE HINDU
TEMPLES OF
PONDA

Above: *The great water tank at the Shri Mangesh Temple is one of Goa's largest. It is probably the oldest feature of the complex*

Below Left: *Safa Shahouri Mosque at Ponda, built in 1560 by Ali Adil Shah, is one of only two mosques of historic interest to have survived in Goa*

Below Right: *This lamp tower, at the Shri Mangesh Temple of Priol, is the most impressive in Goa; examples are rarely found outside the state*

brought from a site only 10 km (6 miles) distant from Cortalim, at approximately the same time as the Mangesh idol, and the present temple was similarly begun in the mid-eighteenth century.

Even for Hindus, the legend of Mahalsa, to whom the temple has been dedicated, is complicated: some believe that the goddess is an incarnation of Laxmi, others that she is a female aspect of Vishnu himself.

A period of expansion and alteration was completed at the temple in 1993, during which the lamp tower was rebuilt, a hall added to the front of the building and, sadly, a 7m (23ft) high *vrindavan* (giant flower pot) the most baroque example in Goa, pointlessly demolished. The ablutions tank, behind the complex, is far less impressive than that at Priol.

Above the central arch of the gateway is the *naubat khana*, where musical instruments, particularly drums, are played during religious ceremonies. Facing the temple is a brass lamp pillar resting on the back of a tortoise, added in 1978. It is surmounted by a Garuda, the winged steed of Vishnu. Here, most roofs are in the form of pink-tiled pyramids; the dome over the sanctuary is the only example, and rather oriental in style.

The columns of the *mandapam* (hall) are of wood, finely carved and decorated, and a sculpted frieze represents the ten incarnations of Vishnu. Peacock tails drape the silver entrance to the shrine, where the Mahalsa idol may clearly be seen.

Shri Laxmi Narasimha Temple

Velinga, where the next temple is situated, lies a short distance south of Mardol, and is again reached by taking a right turn off the main Ponda road.

Although the buildings of the Shri Laxmi Narasimha Temple at Velinga are of no great interest, this temple, another migrant from Salcete, possesses one of the most delightful water tanks in Goa. Fed by a spring, the deep tank is approached from flights of steps.

Enclosing the tank is a range of arched niches for changing purposes; the niches are divided by pilasters, a European feature. Between the two-arched entrances to the tank is a two-storey shrine, with, behind it, a Cosmic Pillar.

Just outside the entrance, set in the hillside, is a short *naubat khana* tower, with the usual musicians' balcony. Apart from the hall extension, most of the structure is eighteenth-century work. Narasimha is a form of Vishnu, in which he appears half man, half lion; the small image of the god was transferred here in 1567.

Four more temples, all close to each other, are reached by continuing 4 km (2.5 miles) southward on the main Ponda road to the village of Farmagudi, and then taking the westbound road (right) at the small roundabout to **Bandora** 1 km (two thirds of a mile) away.

Shri Nagesh Temple

Most of this temple dates from the eighteenth century, although it was founded much earlier. Unlike both the temples already described, the idol was not brought here from elsewhere, but is original to the site. Brightly painted reliefs of gods decorate the lower stages of the short lamp tower.

The large tank (where bathers share the water with fishes) lies to the rear. Set in the wall of the entrance is a black basalt slab, carved with the date 24 December 1413, and an inscription recording that money would be provided for the worship of both Nagesh and Mahalaxmi at Bandora. It may be inferred, therefore, that this temple, and the nearby Shri Mahalaxmi temple, were both founded at that time.

The temple's entrance faces the tank, and a black Nandi bull indicates that Nagesh is an incarnation of Shiva. Just below the ceiling of the *mandapam* hall is a famous wooden frieze, carved and painted with scenes from the Ramayana (the story of Vishnu's incarnation as Rama), and the great Mahabaratha epic. Set in the porches left and right are shrines to Laxminarayana and Ganesh, respectively.

Opposite the latter, in the courtyard, shrines contain *lingam*, one of which depicts the phallic symbol inscribed with a face, and known as a *mukhalingam*. Few other examples are to be found in Goa.

Note on politeness

Similarities between *mukhalinga* (the Hindu idol depicted as a phallus with a face) and the best-selling *Wicked Willy* books or light-hearted promotions for the use of condoms, may strike some western visitors as humourous, but these idols are regarded as deeply religious objects by Hindus, and it would be most impolite to betray amusement.

Shri Mahalaxmi Temple

The road continues in the direction of the village of Queula, and a right turn leads to a valley in which stands Bandora's second temple.

As we have just seen, the proposed worship of Mahalaxmi at Bandora is referred to in the Nagesh temple, and it was probably on this site that the present Shri Mahalaxmi Temple at Bandora was founded in about 1413. Its ancient idol, however, is a migrant from Colva, being transferred here to escape the Portuguese iconoclasts in 1565; presumably it replaced a less popular deity.

Unusually for a Ponda temple, there is no lamp tower, the most significant vertical element being the black basalt Cosmic Pillar. As the domes are shallow and the towers low, the effect is predominantly horizontal; an additional hall emphasises this.

Flanking the entrance to the *mandapam* are paintings of the monkey god Hanuman and the winged Garuda. Below the *mandapam*'s ceiling, a colourful frieze includes scenes from Vishnu's reincarnation as Lord Krishna. The elephant-headed Ganesh guards the carved wooden doors.

Mahalaxmi, who is worshipped in the shrine, is revered throughout much of western India as the supreme female goddess. Incorporated in her headdress may be seen a *lingam,* indicating the strong influence of Shiva.

A pathway leads to the water tank, which is sited further from the temple than is usual. An eighteenth-century house is passed on the way to it, which was built for the Raja of Sunda after he had transferred Ponda's administration to the Portuguese. The Raja lived here under Portuguese protection and the building remains the home of his descendants.

Shri Shantadurga Temple

Return to the road from Farmagudi, turn right and continue towards **Queula** (or Kaule as it is sometimes called). However, instead of turning right towards the village at the intersection, turn left, in the direction of the town of Ponda. A short distance away, on the left, stands Ponda's largest temple.

Not only is the Shri Shantadurga Temple of Queula the largest temple in Ponda, it is also the most visited by worshippers (although not by tourists) in all Goa. The temple is boldly situated on a hill, indicating a basic difference between it and the other Ponda temples already seen.

The Shantadurga Temple, built by Shahurajat in 1738, as proclaimed at the entrance, probably occupies a different site from its simple predecessor, as the god's figure had been brought to Queula from the Old Conquests to escape the Portuguese, and it was usual to conceal such idols in heavily forested valleys.

The courtyard is approached by a flight of steps. Its unusually large size was required so that accommodation could be built around it for the administrators of the temple and the vast number of pilgrims that would flock to it.

A two-colour scheme has been adopted for the complex. The domed, three-stage tower above the sanctuary, and the six-storey lamp tower are both maintained a dazzling white, contrasting strongly with the ochre shades of the remainder. In no other Goan temple is the European baroque influence more strongly apparent.

Seek out the immense chariot (*rath*), elegantly painted in gold and black, which may be standing either in the courtyard or in its shelter. Horses form part of its decoration, but, as with all *rath*s, strong-limbed devotees provide the power to move the heavy vehicle.

An ancient aravali tree is another important feature of the

courtyard; its base is inset with shrines, including a small figure of Bhagavati, an aggressive form of Parvati, Shiva's consort.

Doors to the temple's modern entrance hall and the original vestibule are both beautifully carved and decorated with silver. In the pillared *mandapam*, a superb silver screen surrounds the entrance to the sanctuary, which, although small, is exquisitely decorated, also in silver. Shiva and Vishnu flank the marble image of Shantadurga.

Parvati, Shiva's consort, slayed a demon named Durga and took its name; later, Shanta, meaning peace, was added as a prefix, in

Shri Mahalsa Temple at Mardol

recognition of the goddess's achievement in reconciling Vishnu and Shiva, whose cataclysmic dispute had put the universe in jeopardy.

Shri Ramnath Temple

A thoroughfare lined with shops leads from the base of the temple steps to the Shri Ramnath Temple at Bandora, the final one in the group. Its idol was transferred from Lutolim, in Salcete taluka, and had been worshipped formerly in a temple situated very close to that of the Shantadurga idol previously described. Their proximity to each other once more was, no doubt, divinely inspired.

The entrance hall is an overdominant addition of 1905, but the *mandapam* is sumptuous eighteenth-century work, with a colourful pavement and, above all, an arched sanctuary wall entirely clad in silver. Glorious bas-reliefs cover the surrounds of the arch and its flanking columns, providing some of the most exotic decorative work in all Goa.

The sacred Ramnath image is in the form of a *lingam*, which immediately announces that the dedication is to Shiva, rather than Lord Rama (Vishnu), as some might expect from the name. However, the shrine is shared with Laxminarayana, a joint incarnation of Vishnu and his consort.

Further away from the border with the Old Conquests, Ponda's temples are generally less significant, serving the needs of small villages, rather than pilgrims.

The Safa Shahouri Mosque

North-east of Ponda lies the Safa Shahouri Mosque, one of Goa's only two ancient mosques, and the only non-Christian sixteenth-century building to survive in the state. During the sixteenth century, twenty-seven mosques stood in the Ponda area alone, but the only other historic mosque that now survives in Goa is the **Namazgah** mosque near the town of Bicholim, built in 1683 .

Ponda *taluka* had been controlled, briefly, by Prince Abdullah, a Muslim vassal of the Portuguese, but, in 1560, the army of the Bijapur Sultan Ali Adil Shah recaptured it. Adil Shah commissioned the Safa Shahouri Mosque at Ponda in the same year, probably to emphasise the renewal of Bijapur power in the area.

Little more than the prayer hall and a huge ablutions tank survive, fragments of columns being all that remains of the courtyard.

The square prayer hall is decorated with Bijapuri-style arches; its tiled roof is modern. There is no indication that the mosque was ever domed, nor that it possessed minarets. The building has been repainted recently above the level of its base, which, together with the steeply-pitched roof, was probably dictated by the exigencies of Goa's heavy monsoon. As usual, the building material employed is the local red laterite stone, its carved external detailing gradually fading. Mecca lies to the west of

---

The 'Temples and Spice Plantations' coach tour

This popular coach tour is a relaxing way for the visitor to experience a little of the history and culture of Goa without the hassle of arranging one's own excursion. A hallmark of this tour is the gentle charm and friendliness of the local people, with the very minimum of commercialization.

After passing through Ponda, a road branches northward to **Savoi-Verem**. The day is spent visiting selected temples, which always include the Anant Devasthan Temple sited near Savoi-Verem, an intimate, peaceful temple which even the arrival of a coach party fails to disturb.

India and, therefore, the prayer wall (*mihrab*), with its blind niches, is orientated in that direction.

Ablutions facilities in mosques generally face the entrance to the prayer hall (in this case the west side), but it will be noted that for some reason the water tank here is situated on the south side. Perhaps the lie of the land and the position of a spring made this more convenient. Steps descending to the water have recently been rebuilt, and the tank's general appearance, with arched changing niches, differs little from the bathing tanks in Hindu temples. Architectural similarities between the mosque and its tank indicate that they are contemporary.

Another smaller tank nearby appears to be fed from the main tank, which would necessitate a low level link between them, thus substantiating the alleged danger of swimming underwater in the latter, due to the presence of tunnels.

Anant Devasthan Temple

The temple's pastoral situation contributes greatly to its charm, as does the initial view, looking down on the complex, which is approached by steep steps. Pink-tiled pitched roofs are the chief external feature of the temple, there being no dome or lamp tower. The water tank seems to be regarded primarily as the village swimming pool by the local youngsters.

Within, the colour scheme of the *mandapa* is frankly gaudy, but this contributes to the general gaiety of the atmosphere, with skipping, laughing children expressing natural ease with their religion.

Unusually, visitors are permitted to approach the idol (a contribution to temple maintenance is welcomed), in the form of a black stone, which depicts Anant, the serpent, floating on the Cosmic Ocean, supporting Narayana, an aspect of Vishnu.

A 1,000-year-old image of Vishnu, including all the god's *avatars*, was discovered in the nearby village and is now an

Stylistically, Goa's Hindu temples possess some essential differences from those found elsewhere in India.

Rather than a high, tapering tower (shikara), a shallow dome on a short, octagonal base generally rises above the sanctuary. It seems likely that the multitude of Muslim domes built in Tiswadi prior to the Portuguese conquest inspired this variation, although some experts believe that Goan temples were domed as early as the fourteenth century.

The second major difference is the lamp tower (deepastambha), a free-standing structure, usually octagonal in shape and indented with niches in which lamps are lit during festivals. Only rarely will either of these features be found outside Goa; the finest examples are in Ponda.

Full size figures of elephants flank the Shir Bhagavati Temple at Pernem

The influence of European baroque architecture is apparent in most Goan temples, where pilasters, cornices, balustrades and Classical Orders frequently provide the main decorative features.

In plan, however, Goan temples usually follow the standard Hindu format, with an entrance vestibule (antaralya) followed by a hall (mandapam), which is supported by columns, and a small sanctuary (garbhagriham).

In many of the larger temples, an additional hall has been added recently in front of the vestibule, to accommodate cultural performances; these, unfortunately, tend to give the temple an off-balance appearance.

A rather spindly bush, known as a tulsi, is always found within Hindu complexes. Its derivation is Tulsi, a mistress of Vishnu: she was turned into this plant by Vishnu's jealous consort, Laxmi. The tulsi grows out of a giant plant pot (vrindavan). Some vrindavans are quite simple, but others are extravagantly decorated with colourful ceramics or stone carvings.

A wagon-like chariot, known as a rath, in which the temple's chief idol is borne on major festivals, is found in major temples. It is physically transported by many willing hands.

Ritual ablutions are required of Hindus before entering their temples for prayer, and, to facilitate this, most temples contain a water tank adjacent to the main structure. In Goa's permanently hot climate, cooling off in the tank is a pleasure as well as a duty.

Shoes must be removed by everyone before entering a Hindu temple; fortunately, however, in view of the frequently hot pavement, socks may be kept on. Slip-on footwear is advisable and remember that shorts are not appreciated.

Savoi-Verem spice plantation

Next stop is the Savoi-Verem spice plantation where copious amounts of *feni* are offered prior to lunch, and it is said that some never actually get to view the plantation itself, which is a pity!

A charming young boy or girl is allocated as 'host or hostess' to each visitor, and only a simple souvenir is expected for their solicitous attention — ball-point pens are most welcome.

Not only spices, but fruit, such as pineapple, papaya, jackfruit and mango are seen growing. The afternoon ends, merrily, with everyone being splashed with water — a welcome ceremony in the tropical heat.

important exhibit at Old Goa's Archaeological Museum. Savoi-Verem village is recorded as having been granted to the teacher of one of the early Kadamba rulers in the eleventh century.

Other places of interest

Candola Village

Temple enthusiasts might be able to arrange to see the **Ganesh Temple**, 5 miles (8km) north in the village of Candola, before returning to their hotel.

In spite of his popularity as the son of Shiva, there is only one other temple in Goa where Ganesh is pre-eminent. The original idol is black and rather dilapidated — hardly surprising after 700 years and many changes of venue. It remains in the sanctuary approached by steps, but now stands to one side of a modern version. The idol's first home was in a temple at *Ela*, the village which would later become Old Goa.

From the traces that remain, it is apparent that the Kadamba period provided some of Goa's finest, if not its very finest, architecture. Unfortunately, the temple at **Tambdi Surla** is the only major example to survive, all others having been demolished by subsequent conquerors.

However, those wishing to visit the Bondla Wildlife Sanctuary, in the eastern segment of Ponda, may wish to pause on the way to inspect minor examples of Kadamba temples, in themselves a rarity.

Candepar village

Candepar village, just 5km (3 miles) east of Ponda town on the main road, possesses four sanctuaries, originally cut from the rocky hillside to form 'caves'; later, the surrounding ground was laboriously removed, so that each is now a free-standing structure. The sole decorative external features are the layered slabs, which form the stepped-pyramid *shikaras* surmounting the roofs.

It is believed that the sanctuaries were created in the tenth or eleventh centuries to provide accommodation, at a time when Buddhists were still permitted to follow their religion in the area. If they are Buddhist in origin, then the *shikaras*, a purely Hindu feature, would have been added by the Kadambas to existing structures.

Three of the sanctuaries have two chambers, the fourth just one. Sockets indicate that each shrine was once fitted with a door, but none have survived or been replaced.

Within the sanctuaries, niches and pegs for hanging garments have been cut out of the rock. Simple, lotus-petal ceilings, are in typical Kadamba style and would certainly have been built at the same time as the *shikaras*.

Opa village

A road leads south from Candepar to Opa village, a few minutes drive away. Nearby, on the edge of a tributary of the Mandovi river, stands a more impressive **Kadamba Temple**. This was built in the thirteenth century and has been sympathetically kept in good order. The temple, dedicated to Shiva, is still in use.

Structurally of laterite, basalt has also been used for certain features, such as columns and door frames. Externally, the *shikara* follows the usual tapering format prefered by the Kadambas. However, the roof lantern, surmounted by a cupola, is an unusual feature for the period and probably a much later addition.

A small entrance hall and an even smaller sanctuary comprise the interior, the chief features of which are two cusped niches with, between them, the carved frame of the sanctuary door. Shiva is represented by a small, metal-clad *lingam*.

Bondla Wildlife Sanctuary

Returning to the main road and turning right, a branch left forks to Usgao village, from where a narrow road snakes uphill through forests towards the entrance to the Bondla Wildlife Sanctuary. This is one of Goa's three wildlife sanctuaries, and only here are visitors likely to see fauna of exceptional interest.

Encompassing just 8 sq km (3 square miles), it must be said that Bondla resembles more a naturalistic zoo than a true sanctuary, as the more exotic animals are unable to leave their, admittedly large, enclosures: leopard, bison and sambhar deer are the star attractions, but not tiger.

For some reason, monkeys in Goa are more nervous than their brethren in other parts of India, and keep well away from human settlements. Here, however, they are fairly numerous and offer many visitors their best chance of seeing a wild monkey in Goa.

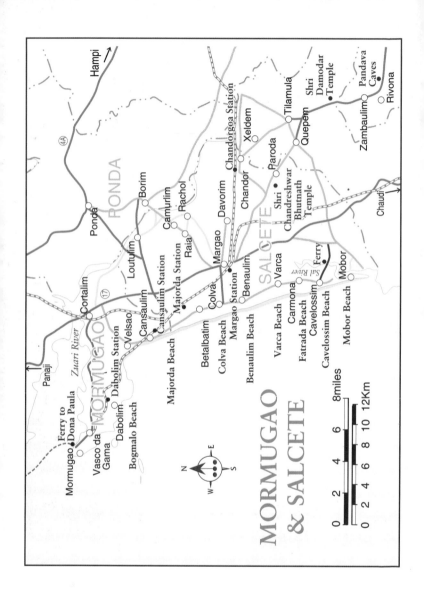

Opposite: One of the Great Hotels of the World,
the Four Seasons Leela Beach Hotel

5 Mormugao & Salcete

The Southern Beaches

Forming one unbroken beach 25 km (16 miles) long, the coastline of Salcete Taluka accommodates a high proportion of the holidaymakers who visit Goa. Lively beach bars/restaurants proliferate near the villages, and it will not take holidaymakers long to select their favourites. Some spend many happy hours strolling from bar to bar, occasionally braving the swell to cool off in the azure sea; others traverse the whole beach by motorbike, an invigorating, if rather expensive, experience!

Many hotels near the beach have their own pools, which non-residents are welcome to use for either the price of a drink or a fee.

Further beach interest is provided by fishermen: painting and repairing their boats, anchoring them offshore, or pulling in the nets.

In 1917, the wide northern peninsula of Salcete was sliced off to form Mormugao *taluka*, for easier administrative purposes. Goa's airport, **Dabolim,** is situated in Mormugao, as is the state's largest and most heavily populated town, Vasco da Gama.

Bogmalo Beach

Bogmalo Beach, dominated by the **Bogmalo Beach Park Plaza Resort Hotel,** lies just 2 km (1.25 miles) south of the airport.

The hotel is the only multistorey building to overlook a beach in all Goa, its construction being immediately greeted with horror by most Goans. This led to controls on the height, design and distance from the beach of all shoreline buildings; fortunately, these regulations have been strictly enforced.

However, many visitors to Goa are now so used to the concrete excesses of international beach resorts that they will be little disturbed by the hotel, particularly as its lower storeys are now almost completely hidden from sight by palm trees planted in front of it. Upgrading of all rooms will take place in 1998/9.

Surprisingly, in view of the existence of this luxury hotel, the prices at Bogmalo's beach bars and restaurants are most reasonable, and there are few beach vendors to bother the holidaymaker. This is presumably because Bogmalo is the nearest good beach to Vasco da Gama and, in consequence, the majority of visitors are local.

Alternative accommodation on the beach is provided by **Joet's Guesthouse** (13 rooms), with a very smart terrace for eating and drinking.

Colva Beach

The great Colva Beach commences east of Bogmalo and for easier identification purposes, the various sections now take the name of the nearest local village.

Most of Colva Beach is similar in character to the great northern stretch of sand between Sinquerim Beach and Baga Beach. As practically its entire length is backed by flat, low-lying ground, usually cultivated as paddy-fields, there is no backdrop of hills to be seen once the Mormugao peninsula has been left, or until the Western Ghat mountains are sighted from its southern extremity.

From **Velsao,** a road follows the coastline, linking the fishing villages, all of which lie approximately one mile inland; they are described from north to south, together with their beaches.

Velsao and Cansaulim

Neither Velsao nor Cansaulim villages, both still in Mormugao, are particularly noteworthy, but visitors who are staying in the area on 6 January will enjoy the **Epiphany Festival** of Reis Magos, which is celebrated at Cansaulim, in addition to Reis Magos and Chandor. Cansaulim's railway station, on the line between Margao and Vasco da Gama, is situated nearer to a good beach than any other in Goa.

Majorda

Majorda Beach marks the entry to Salcete *taluka*. This formed part of the Old Conquests, and Christianity is still by far the most important religion, over 70 per cent of the population being Roman Catholic. Many churches, but very few temples, will therefore be found in the region.

Majorda's eighteenth-century church, dedicated to **Our Lady Mother of God**, stands on the site of a temple; it replaced an earlier building destroyed by the invading Marathas in 1738.

Like Cansaulim, **Majorda** village also has a railway station, but from here the track moves gradually away from the coast until, at **Margao**, 5 km (3 miles) distant, it makes an abrupt eastward turn, continuing inland to the state border.

The **Hotel Goa Penta**, opened in 1993, and the much larger **Majorda Beach Resort**, both four-star rated, provide luxury accommodation a short stroll from the village towards the sea.

Betalbatim

Betalbatim, the next village, takes its name from Betal, one of the most violent forms of Shiva. A headless figure of Betal, dating from the twelfth century, which once stood in the temple, was found in the village; it is now exhibited in Old Goa's Archaeological Museum.

Colva

The section of Colva Beach that lies just a mile from Colva village is the nearest stretch of sand to **Margao**, by far the largest and most populous town in Salcete, and its development owes more to this factor than Goa's popularity with tourists. Visitors will find, therefore, that on Colva's own beach, especially at weekends and festivals, Indians greatly outnumber foreigners.

Motorbike hire

The entire length of Colva Beach may be explored on motorbikes, which their owners lease by the hour.

Although they are very popular with tourists, rates initially demanded are usually outrageously high and so should be negotiated firmly downward.

From Colva, southward, there are several pitches behind the beach from where motorbikes can be hired.

Between the beach and the village, the road is lined by a multitude of thatched shacks, providing food, drink, clothing and, of course, souvenirs. Nevertheless, this is still very much a fisherman's beach, and the section to the left, as the sands are approached from the path, aromatically emphasises this fact, it is here that the fishermen store their great nets.

Fishing boats are always bobbing on the swell, a short distance from the shore, and nowhere else in Goa are they seen in such profusion. Many will find this emphasis on fishing, and the predominance of locals, a refreshing change from Goa's other tourist beaches.

However, it appears to have frightened away developers of upper-grade hotels, as most of Colva's accommodation tends to be rather basic. A stream runs parallel with the sands, traversed by small bridges. Of the numerous bar/ restaurants, **Joe Cons** is extremely popular. **Tequila's** and **Longhuino's** are also recommended.

Colva Church

The parish church, **Our Lady of Mercy**, is the only interesting building in **Colva** village. Founded in 1630, the church was rebuilt in the eighteenth century. The Greek symbol for Jesus, IHS, is inscribed in the roundel below the pediment, indicating the

The Menino Jesus – Corva Church

On view one day every month, the Menino (Boy) Jesus figure, incorporated in the chancel's north altarpiece, is honoured annually by a *Fama* (Fame) celebration on the second Monday in October, when it is clad in sumptuous clothes and jewels, paraded around the church, and bathed, before being returned to the altar.

The figure was made in 1836 to replace its predecessor, which had been brought to Colva from West Africa by a Jesuit missionary when he became its vicar in 1648.

Soon the statue gained a reputation for healing, becoming the object of great devotion and the recipient of gifts, including precious jewels. When religious orders were banished from Goa in 1834, Colva's vicar had to leave, and the Menino Jesus, plus its treasures, was transferred to Rachol Seminary.

For some reason, a diamond ring was overlooked, remaining at Colva, and this is displayed on one of the statue's fingers during the festival.

Parishioners who have recovered from sickness during the year, present the figure with sections of the human body made of wax. These symbolize the locations of their particular ailments, and are purchased from a stall outside the church specially set up for the day: profits go to the Menino charity.

Above: *The Menezes Braganza House at Chandor*

Below: *The Park Plaza Hotel at Bogmalo Beach is the only hotel in Goa to overlook the sea*

influence of the Jesuits. Entered from its cloister, internally all is baroque, with brilliant colours, swirling canopies and gilded altarpieces.

Benaulim Beach

Colva Beach merges almost imperceptibly with **Benaulim Beach** to the south; the fishing boats have disappeared — and so have the crowds. Once again, no high-grade hotels currently exist here, but **L'Amour Beach Resort**, overlooking the beach, has a good reputation.

Many Goan place names were slightly altered by the Portuguese to aid pronunciation; Benaulim had formerly been called *Bannali*, meaning 'where the arrow fell'. The arrow in question was the mythical shaft aimed by Parashurama from the mountains to define the extent of the new land of Goa.

Benaulim Church

Benaulim's church, **St John the Baptist**, located some distance from the village, is unusual in Salcete as it occupies a hillside position. Apparently, its predecessor had stood between the village and the sea; it may have been felt that a higher site would be preferable, due to the risk of flooding during the monsoon.

The church is not large, but a visit is well worth making if staying in the area. There is the usual profusion of baroque detailing and, in the nave, an appealing 'primitive' bas-relief of St Christopher crossing the river

with the infant Jesus. The saint's head is cocked at a jaunty angle.

Fr Josep Vaz (1651-1711) was born in the village and baptized in the chapel below the choir. He is revered in Goa for his efforts to encourage the Portuguese clerical authorities to permit native Goans to enter the priesthood. Set in extensive grounds, the luxurious Taj Exotica, planned to open for the 1998/9 season, lies back from Benaulim Beach.

Varca Beach

A short distance to the south, the three-star **Resorte de Goa** hotel, situated close to the sea, marks the beginning of Varca Beach. A road leads inland from the hotel to **Varca** church, with its splendid façade. Varca village, almost a mile further south, is of little interest, although **Pedro's** bar, on the road to the beach, is a popular venue.

Carmona and Cavelossim

Both the next two villages, Carmona and Cavelossim, have attractive eighteenth-century churches: **Our Lady of Help**, and **The Holy Cross**, respectively.

Fatrada and Mobor Beach

Much of the coastal area between Cavelossim and Mobor Beach is now occupied by four- and five-star hotels, which together provide the most prestigious group in Goa: **Dona Sylvia** at Cavelossim Beach, and the **Holiday Inn** and **Four Seasons Leela Beach Resort**, situated close to each other where Cavelossim

Beach merges with Mobor Beach.

The Four Seasons Leela Beach Hotel, a member of the 'Leading Hotels in the World' group, is laid out to resemble a Mediterranean village, where guests occupy

---

Mobor fishing village

Walking southward along **Mobor Beach**, holidaymakers are soon replaced by local villagers laying out thousands of tiny fish for drying on the sand, to the acquisitive interest of black-headed gulls which perform frantic aerobatics as they are approached. The pungent fish are intended for animal fodder, not human consumption. At this point, the wide inlet of the River Sal is reached, and its west shore may be followed to **Mobor** village, in the centre of the narrow isthmus between river and sea.

---

luxuriously-fitted bungalows, most with canal views. Already-luxurious accommodation was upgraded in 1997/8 and the tariff is expected to pinpoint the business and super-rich market.

The most southerly section of the beach is known as Betul Beach, which confuses many as Betul village lies on the opposite bank of the river and can only be reached by boat. A particular delight of this

area is that the Western Ghat mountains sweep down to the sea a short distance away. A holiday here will naturally be more expensive than in most other Goan resorts, due to the luxury facilities and high standard of cuisine provided.

Unless excursions are taken, the peaceful, 'international' atmosphere will preclude visitors returning home with a strong impression of having been to India.

Inland excursions

Most excursions to inland Salcete pass through **Margao**, the chief town of the *taluka*, and are described in the following pages.

In addition, however, a visit to **Palolem Beach** in Canacona *taluka* by fishing boat from various points in Salcete is highly recommended. The mountainous, indented coastline passed is superb and the beach at Palolem, generally regarded as Goa's most idyllic.

Margao

Although its population does not approach that of Vasco da Gama, **Margao**, Salcete's administrative centre, is still regarded as Goa's second most important town after Panaji.

Before the Muslims arrived, Margao boasted many splendid temples, but all were, of course, demolished by the Portuguese when Salcete was incorporated in the Old Conquests. Historically, Margao's importance stemmed from its central position as a distributor of agricultural produce for a wide area, a position which it still maintains.

Most will arrive at Margao by motor vehicle: buses are more convenient than trains, as they are far more frequent and deposit passengers in the town centre, whereas the railway station lies to the south. However, with the opening of the Konkan railway line, trains will greatly reduce the journey time to both the northern beaches and to Canacona.

Jorge Barreto Park area

Regarded as the hub of Margao, Jorge Barreto Park is a rectangular, planted area, its south end overlooked by the Municipal Building, a colonial structure with arcades and balconies, completed in 1905, and accommodating the public library.

The market

Immediately east of the Municipal Building, framed by conventional shops, lies Margao's famous market, only matched in Goa by Mapusa's. Those wishing to purchase Indian ceramics or clothing will find prices here lower than anywhere else, subject, of course, to the usual hard bargaining.

However, the extravagant displays of fish and fruit are perhaps the market's biggest attraction. It is at Margao's market that the new season's famous Goan mangoes are first offered to the public in March.

Abbe Faria Street

Buses usually deposit visitors at the north-east corner of the park,

The Church

The Church of the Holy Spirit was founded in 1565, on the site of a great, pagoda-like structure, the Temple of Damodar, then Margao's most important building.

This had been erected on the spot where assassins hired by a jealous suitor had murdered Macaji Damodar and his bride on their wedding day. Damodar, a local youth, must have been extremely popular, for his violent death soon acquired legendary aspects, and the Margaons built a great temple in his honour.

Like so many Goan temples in the Old Conquests, it was demolished by the iconoclastic Diego Rivas on the instructions of Goa's first archbishop, Dom Caspar Leao Pereira, and the predecessor of the present church constructed on the site. The temple's *linga* survived, however, as it had been transferred, just in time, to the Sanguem/Quepem border, at **Zambaulim** village, where it is still venerated.

The Hindu gods quickly took their revenge, as Muslim raiders destroyed the church soon after it had been consecrated. Rebuilt quickly, its replacement was similarly razed to the ground by another

of the Holy Spirit - Margao

Muslim attack in 1579, and does not appear to have been replaced until the present church was constructed in 1675.

A Jesuit seminary had been opened alongside the second building in 1574, but this was also destroyed by the Muslims, and its function transferred to a safer location at Rachol, where a new seminary was built within the walls of the existing fort.

Interestingly, only the west façade and the façades of both transepts are plastered and painted; elsewhere the walls are of undecorated laterite. No doubt, this two-tone scheme was dictated by economic factors, but the painted areas are always kept in pristine condition. The west façade is entirely symmetrical and extremely baroque, with rounded windows, pilasters, pedimented architraves, scrolls and balustraded towers.

The flanking towers which, as usual, are set back from the rest of the façade, are surmounted by flat domes, their lanterns topped by cupolas. This architectural feature became popular in Goan churches and temples during the eighteenth and nineteenth centuries, and appears to have made its first appearance here.

Recessed in a balustraded niche in the centre of the third stage of the façade is a bas-relief of Our Lady surrounded by the apostles (**binoculars are an advantage**); the carving is in typical Goan naïve style. On the central pediment, a further relief, of a dove, represents the Holy Spirit.

To enter the church, proceed through the archway on the south side, which leads to a courtyard formed by houses built to accommodate members of the clergy. The nave is unusually high, with a coffered vault. In the transepts, the altarpieces dedicated to St Peter and St Michael are outstanding examples of Indian baroque carving.

The sanctuary is framed by Corinthian columns which are linked by a delicate, curved frieze around the arch. Within, the high altar's gilded reredos comprises reliefs: the central panel, as in the façade of the church, illustrates the Virgin Mary with the Apostles; again, the dove of the Holy Spirit is seen above. Beneath the choir, an altarpiece depicts the wedding of Mary and Joseph.

and an immediate left turn leads to Margao's most famous street, Abbe Faria, stretching northward as a continuation of the park's west throughfare. Miraculously, most of the colonial-style houses from the eighteenth and nineteenth centuries have survived, although some of them are desperately in need of maintenance, particularly paintwork. However, carved woodwork is a constant delight.

Towards the end of the street, on the left, facing Subraya Naik Road, a room in an unpretentious bungalow has been adapted to accommodate the small temple of Damodar. Those who have visited Amsterdam may be reminded of the 'hidden' churches created in private houses for Roman Catholic worship during the period of Protestant repression.

Church Square

Directly ahead, Church Square, formed by the Church of the Holy Spirit and clusters of colonial residences, is Margao's most picturesque sector. In its centre, beside a great mango tree, stands a monumental cross, which predates the church behind it by a century. Built of lime-plastered laterite, the cross is painted annually, but even so its detail is gradually fading. The design is essentially Baroque, although some Hindu features have been incorporated, particularly in the finials. Of the many crosses of this type in Goa, there is none finer.

Sat Burnzam Gor

A short street curves from the south-east corner of Church Square to Agostinho Lourenco Street. On the right-hand side, at the point where this becomes San Joaquim Road, stands Sat Burnzam Gor, one of Goa's most splendid residences. The name refers to seven (sat) roofs, but now there are only three, two bays flanking the remaining structure on each side having been demolished. The Viceroy's secretary, Inacio Silva, commissioned the house about 1790 and his descendants still live here. Restrained in design, each bay is identical, the vertical emphasis creating a pleasing rhythm.

Unfortunately, it is seldom possible to visit the house. Most of the more important rooms have survived, including the great salon, where two hundred guests were often received; the room has since been subdivided. Also retained is the great staircase and the family chapel, one of the first examples in Goa where private Mass was permitted; it extends into the small courtyard at the rear.

If time permits, some may wish to take a taxi to **Mount Church**, rebuilt in 1820, from where there are impressive hilltop views over Margao to the sea.

Eating out

Recommended restaurants in Margao are **Longhuino's Food Affair** (Indian and Chinese), **Galings** (Chinese) and **Kandeel** (Goan specialities at economical prices).

Those visiting Ponda's temples from the Colva Beach area will pass through Margao, crossing the River Zuari by the Borim bridge. The temples will then be seen in reverse order to that previously given.

Northern Salcete: Rachol and Loutulim

Four miles (6.5 km) north-east of Margao, a turning right from the main road at **Raia** village leads to Rachol.

Rachol Seminary

It is on this fortified hill that Margao's College of All Saints was re-established in 1580, following its destruction by Muslim raiders the previous year. Obviously a less vulnerable site, little of the original protective fort has survived, but the seminary itself has a fortress-like aspect, which is probably intentional. The Jesuit seminary was renamed to commemorate Ignatius Loyola, founder of their Order, but, on the expulsion of the Jesuits from Goa in 1759, its name was altered to The Good Shepherd.

Rachol has always been renowned for its high standard of learning; one of India's first printing presses was set up here to print a bible in the local language, which had been translated by an English resident, Father Thomas Stephens. Stephens arrived at Goa in 1579, and may have been the first Englishman to have visited the Indian sub-continent. Over one hundred young men from many parts of India still receive training for the priesthood at Rachol, which involves an arduous seven-year course.

Apart from an extension in the late nineteenth century, most of the present structure dates from the rebuilding of 1606 and some of the domestic buildings constructed around the seminary's main courtyard may usually be viewed.

The entrance hall is approached by a staircase, at the top of which crouches a headless Nandi bull, discovered during excavations in the main courtyard, and indicates that Rachol had once been the site of a temple to Shiva. Within, the hall's vault is supported by one great pier; the seminary's hallmark of delicate murals is continued on its walls.

The main courtyard is enclosed by the church and three domestic ranges with corridors on both floors. The columns in the courtyard originally formed part of a vine terrace. Water cisterns lie beneath the courtyard's pavement, and may be approached by narrow steps. It was near here that the Nandi bull was discovered, and it is thought that the cisterns are remnants of the temple's ablutions tank.

Other areas of interest are the great hall on the first floor, in which are displayed paintings of Goan archbishops and the 20-year-old Portuguese King Sebastião, who founded this seminary at Margao in 1574; ten years later, Sebastiao was killed in a pointless battle with the Moors in North Africa. Located in the block right of the church is the Museum of Christianity (closed 1-2.30pm).

The church at Rachol

The church is still dedicated to St Ignatius Loyola. Relics of Constantine the Great were brought from Rome in 1782 and inserted in the altarpiece immediately left of the entrance; they include pieces of bone and a small flask, which is alleged to have once contained a sample of the first Christian Roman Emperor's blood. The altar is dedicated to (Saint) Constantine, and a figure of him in military uniform is incorporated in the reredos.

Another reredos features the Boy Jesus figure taken from Colva, which was reputed to possess miraculous healing powers prior to being brought here in 1834. Projecting from the south wall of the nave is the sumptuous pulpit. The reredos of the high altar is a splendid, gilded piece, set in an apse and embellished with figures of saints. It is reminiscent of the high altar's reredos in Old Goa's cathedral, with which it is contemporary.

The walls of the chancel are decorated with cartouches depicting scenes from the lives of the saints. Niches within the sacristy display small sculptures of various figures. The ancient organ pipes, the oldest outside Europe, were brought from Lisbon in the late sixteenth century and are still in use. A long first-floor corridor

Opposite: The best place to relax after an exhausting morning on the beach

leads to the choir, and is known as the **Corredor des Patriarcas;** its murals depict famous saints who founded religious orders. A doorway leads from the corridor to the small Archbishop's Gallery.

Rachol Fort

Rachol Fort, built by the Adil Shahs, was taken from them by the Hindu Vijayanagars in 1520, and presented to the Portuguese in return for promised support against the Muslims. Although frequently besieged, the fort never fell to invaders during its Portuguese ownership, as many as a hundred cannon being employed in its defence.

With the eastward expansion of Portuguese Goa in the eighteenth century, the fort no longer stood on the border, and its strategic importance ended. Abandoned in 1842, the building became ruinous, and little survives apart from some crumbling walls. There is, however, an interesting stone archway composed of red, yellow and white bands.

Our Lady of the Snows

On the bank of the River Zuari, just below the seminary, stands the church of **Our Lady of the Snows** in Rachol village.

Two interesting reminders of local clashes between the Portuguese and Hindus are seen within: one tomb slab commemorates Diego Rodrigues (who died in 1577), the enthusiastic destroyer of temples, while another, set in the steps to the chancel, indicates the first burial site of five Jesuit missionaries murdered by devout Hindus at Candolim in 1583. Their remains were transferred to the College of St. Paul in Old Goa in 1597 and then to the cathedral in 1907. A painting in the chancel graphically depicts their deaths.

Loutulim

A return to Raia village, and a right turn on the main road, continues the route to Ponda. However, a left turn off this road, just after the next village of Camurlim, leads to one of Goa's most delightful villages, **Loutulim**, famous for its exceptional wealth of colonial domestic architecture.

The centre of Loutulim is its square, at one end of which stands the intensely baroque parish church, a single tower giving the façade a slightly off-balanced appearance. It is, however, the former residences of Portuguese administrators which are of chief interest; some are open to visitors from time to time. (Check details with a Tourist Information Office.)

Roque Caetan Miranda House

A tree-lined lane leads from one corner of the square to the balconied **Roque Caetan Miranda House**, founded in 1815.

A large salon occupies the entire frontage of the top storey; its gleaming, polished wood floor and glass chandeliers, imported from Europe, being contemporary with the building. The chairs are finely carved and incorporate the initials of the original owner, RCM, in their design. Most of the ground floor accommodates the splendid hall, a central staircase and a large chapel.

Miranda House

Located a short distance away from the square is the Miranda House (not to be confused with the building just described), one of the oldest residences in Goa to survive, as it was constructed very early in the eighteenth century or even, possibly, towards the end of the seventeenth century. Only the small iron balconies and low balustraded wall to the ground floor terrace relieve the severity of the façade, which is austerely classical in style. This may be visited by telephoning its owner, Mario Miranda in advance ☎ 777022. Mario is a cartoonist of international standing and many examples of his work are displayed throughout the house.

The upper floor consists of a large banqueting room, at either end of which there is access to the library and the main bedroom. A private chapel, the salon, and further bedrooms are on the ground floor. Although this arrangement is unusual, the common practice in such houses of constructing deep verandahs overlooking an inner courtyard garden is followed.

Salvador Costa House

Another building of importance, situated just outside Loutulim, is the Salvador Costa House. This is fronted by a shady verandah, its decorative fretwork providing a strong 'Indian' feature. The house was inherited by two of the owner's descendants and has, therefore, been subdivided to provide separate dewllings.

On returning to the main road, follow the direction left to Ponda or right to Margao and the coast.

Chandor, Zambaulim, Rivona & Chandranath Hill

This excursion will particularly appeal to those interested in Goa's earliest history, as it includes the site of Chandrapura, Goa's first capital, the ancient Chandreshwar Bhutnath Temple, and the sixth-century Buddhist caves at Rivona. Visitors staying in the area at the time, should not miss the Reis Magos Festival, celebrated at Chandor on 6 January.

It is important that the driver knows exactly where the following sites are located, as few visitors make this journey. Only at Quepem are restaurants available, and a packed lunch is advisable.

Chandor village

Chandor village, centred on its large square, lies just 5 km (3 miles) to the east of Margao (take the second turning left after Davolim village). It may also be reached via Chandorgoa railway station if more convenient.

The village church, **Our Lady of Bethlehem**, was built by Jesuits in 1645, but its façade collapsed in 1949 and has been rebuilt. As usual, the church occupies the site of a former temple, demolished by the Portuguese in 1567.

Around the cross in the square, the **Reis Magos Epiphany Festival** is celebrated on 6 January by a fair and the traditional procession. Chandor is one of only three locations in Goa where this festival is celebrated.

Many are surprised at the unusually large dimensions of the square, believing that they were dictated by the requirements of the Reis Magos fair. In fact, the great length has resulted from the need to accommodate the twenty-four-bay façade of the Menezes Braganza House, which occupies an entire side. It is now open to the public on a regular basis, but check times with Tourist Information Office in Margao.

Menezes Braganza House

The Menezes Braganza family has occupied the house since it was built, in much more modest form, in the late sixteenth century; its members were then Hindu, but later converted to Roman Catholicism. In the eighteenth century, the house acquired most of its present dimensions, however, a further extension took place early in the nine-teenth century.

Cusped upper sections of the French windows are filled with stained glass. The windows of the house that face the road open on to small iron balconies, which are delicately cast in a floral pattern. Pilasters divide the bays but, these apart, there is little decoration externally. No doubt the shallow roof, supported by brackets, which shades the upper floor windows, is a later feature — at least it is tiled and not made of utilitarian corrugated iron as is frequently the case.

The owners of great houses in Goa appear to have relished symmetry; no matter how large the building, the entrance is always placed centrally and the staircase rises immediately from the hallway beyond. All the important rooms in this building are on the first floor, the ground floor rooms accommodating the kitchen, storage areas and servants' quarters. The floors of the reception rooms are of marble — expensive, but much cooler than the usual wood.

On either side of the stairwell are two separate garden courtyards, a unique feature necessitated by the unusual extent of the building. French windows on this side lead to an extremely long open corridor rather than balconies.

The great salon, the most splendid room in the house, is remarkably cool. Lit by European chandeliers, it is sparsely furnished with eighteenth-century settees, their unusual design

Chandrapura

The site of *Chandrapura*, not excavated until 1929, lies 2 km (1.25 miles) from Chandor's square, as is indicated by a large sign.

Pottery discovered in the area indicates that a settlement existed here around 200BC. A copper plate engraved with an edict by a Bhoja king in the third or fourth century AD, the oldest example of the written word in Goa, was also found nearby. It is contemporary with the excavated stone walls of the fortress and the brick foundations of the temple which lay within their protection; these are the most ancient structural traces of buildings so far discovered in Goa.

The temple would have been dedicated to Shiva, as the great Nandi bull, headless and damaged, which once again guards the site of the temple's entrance, was also found here during the 1929 excavations. It is judged to be seventh century work and, like the fortress and temple, may have been destroyed by Tughluq's Muslim invaders when they allegedly sacked *Chandrapura* in 1327, slaughtering its inhabitants.

The name of *Chandrapura* possibly honours Chandragupta Maurya, who ruled in the fourth century BC, and was the father of India's great Buddhist king Ashoka. The town may have been apparently based on contemporary French styles. Some of the family's most prized possessions are displayed in the small anteroom approached from the end of the salon. Other rooms of note are the baroque chapel, the banqueting hall, and the library.

Luis de Menezes Braganza (1878-1938), a newspaper proprietor, is the most renowned member of the family, due to his popular efforts to promote social justice and Goan independence; it was he who was chiefly responsible for creating the library of more than 5,000 books, the most extensive private collection in Goa.

The Shri Damodar Temple at Zambaulim

From Chandor village, take the road that runs south eastward, passing the villages of Xeldem and Tilamola, both in Quepem *taluka*. Do not turn right at Tilamola in the direction of Quepem town, but continue ahead to the Shri Damodar Temple at Zambaulim, which lies just inside the Sanguem *taluka* border. The total distance is little over 10 km (6 miles).

The present temple was built between 1951 and 1972, replacing what was mostly a nineteenth-century building, part of which had become structurally unsound. It houses the **Damodar Macaji** idol, brought here from the Margao 'pagoda' in 1567 to escape Portuguese attention.

It is of particular interest at Zambaulim to observe how the architects have simplified traditional elements in Hindu design for modern needs. An ancient tree provides the central axis for what is basically a symmetrical layout. Marble, in various colours, has been used to great effect throughout, particularly on the sanctuary wall.

The Shiva *lingam* of Damodar, brought from Margao, can be seen in its silver shrine to the left of the sanctuary; however, a black stone representation of Laxminarayana in the shrine, right, is almost equally venerated. While the usual Goan domes have been dispensed

a territorial capital at that time, but it certainly became the capital of the area now known as Goa in the late sixth century, and remained so until the Kadamba dynasty transferred to *Gowapuri* in 1052.

It must be said that the dense woodland, which now covers the area, makes it hard to imagine that this is the centre of what was once a great, fortified town. A further surprise is to learn that much of *Chandrapura's* prominence emanated from its position as an inland port, sited on a tributary of the Zuari and navigable from the sea by all but the largest craft until the nineteenth century.

with in favour of more 'Indian' *shikaras*, ogee domes may be seen surmounting the two shrines outside the courtyard, which have been retained from the earlier temple.

Pandava Caves

The road continues one mile further south to Rivona. After the shops have been passed, follow the short lane, left, which leads to the small **'Pandava' Caves**.

The interest of the two caves at Rivona is chiefly their situation and the fact that they are Buddhist survivals, rare in Goa. It is believed that the caves were hewn out of the laterite rock by Buddhist monks in the seventh century, a date corroborated by a headless Buddha from the same period found on the site. At the time, it was difficult for Buddhists to pursue their religion unimpeded, and the remoteness of the region, plus its constant supply of fresh, spring water, no doubt attracted them.

All external 'construction' was added to the original simple excavation by Hindus after the Buddhists had vacated the cave. Steps descend to a small, ventilated room, its well fed by a spring. Access to a second room at the same level has since been blocked.

An alternative entrance to this cave is approached by steps that lead directly downhill from the left-hand side of the main entrance. Outside stands a carved figure of Hanuman, the monkey god, believed to be sixteenth-century Vijayanagar work. An overhang of rock protects this entrance, from which the room already seen can be reached by struggling through a low gap in the wall — possibly an emergency escape outlet.

Enthusiasts may wish to visit the second cave, although there is not much to be seen. It lies just above the valley floor and is approached by a lengthy path descending from the opposite side of the road. The cave has a wide opening and a raised dais, which suggests that it may have served as a temple, with the Buddha's figure, already referred to, seated on the dais.

The Chandreshwar Bhutnath Temple at Parvath

The main road from Rivona to Margao passes through the town of **Quepem** (of little interest to visitors) and continues to **Paroda** village, nestling beneath Chandranath Hill. A road branching left winds up the hill, ending at the hamlet of Parvath. From here, rough-hewn steps lead to the summit. Note that the climb might prove too much for the elderly, or young children.

The Chandreshwar Bhutnath Temple at Parvath is dramatically sited in a clearing at the 370m (1,213ft) summit of the hill, which is the highest in the region; however, the surrounding trees preclude extensive views. It appears that **Chandranath Hill** has long been a holy site, as remnants of several temples have been discovered.

A predecessor of the temple is recorded as existing by the fifth century BC and this is, therefore, one of Goa's oldest foundations. Its present structure was built in the seventeenth century, gleaming white, with pink tiled roofs. Beside the only tree permitted to grow within the clearing stands a short lamp tower of the earlier type.

It will be noticed that the domed tower, rising above the sanctuary, is unusually high for a Goan temple. As already mentioned, the temple at Chandor village, which lies a similar short distance from the Quepem border, was ruthlessly demolished in 1567 by the Portuguese, who did not relax their religious intolerance until the eighteenth century. So why was this temple, also within the Salcete border, permitted to remain? Its prominent tower could hardly have been missed. The question will probably never be answered.

The temple has two chariots (*raths*) for transporting idols during festivals; these are usually housed in the rather ugly sheds which stand outside the complex. Figures are painted in subtle colours on the columns of the *mandapa* (hall), additional decoration being provided by the frieze of religious themes running below the ceiling.

A Nandi bull crouches protectively in front of the sanctuary's entrance, indicating, of course, that the temple is dedicated to Shiva, represented here by a 'face' *mukhalinga* which, like the sanctuary itself, has been carved out of the rock: both are extremely ancient.

It has been suggested that Chandreshwar (Lord of the Moon), the name by which Shiva is worshipped here, was the original source of all the 'Chandra' names in the area, rather than Chandragupta Maurya. Bhutnath, the second dedication of the temple, refers to another aspect of Shiva (Lord of the Spirits), which is worshipped in a small subsidiary temple outside the main entrance. Shiva's *linga* is in the form of an uncut slab of rock.

6 Sanguem & Canacona

Sanguem

Sanguem is Goa's largest province, its eastern border marking the boundary between Goa and Karnataka state. Due to its distance from the beaches and its mountainous nature, few holidaymakers visit Sanguem *taluka,* which is a great pity as they miss Goa's greatest natural wonder, the Dudhsagar waterfalls, and its most outstanding building, the Shri Mahadeva Temple at Tambdi Surla.

Dudhsagar Waterfalls

As may be imagined, apart from the monsoon period itself, the Dudhsagar Waterfalls are at their most impressive in the period that follows it (October to December), but even as late as April they are still worth seeing. Take a swimming costume and towel in the hotter months, as a cool-off in the

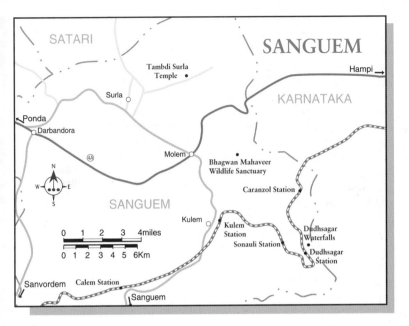

pool below the falls will provide welcome relief from the soaring temperatures, which are little reduced by the altitude.

Getting there

At the time of writing, conversion of the Margao to Dudshagar railtrack from metre to wide gauge had only been completed as far as Kulem, and financial problems had resulted in the scheme coming to a standstill. Until the work is completed, visitors are taken from Kulem to the waterfalls by four-wheel-drive vehicles.

Dudhsagar Falls are India's highest, and as there are no roads or villages in the area it is fortunate

Opposite: The small but exquisite Shri Mahadeva Temple at Tambdi Surla

that all trains on Goa's east/west railway line (normally) halt on the bridge which bisects the cataracts. The two-hour rail journey from Margao to Dudhsagar involves a very long day for tourists based on the northern beaches, However, the new Konkan railway, providing a rapid link between Margao and north and south Goa, is likely to mitigate this.

An alternative for those with a car will be to drive to Kulem railway station and take the train from there to Dudhsagar, a forty-five minute journey. The road via Ponda is preferable. If an early start is made, it will be possible to visit Tambdi Surla Temple and the Bhagwan Mahaveer Wildlife Sanctuary (briefly) before continuing by a later train to Dudhsagar.

131

Travel tips

Travellers must be certain that there is no confusion between Kulem (sometimes spelt Kolem or even Colem) and Calem, the station which precedes it. The only stop between Kulem and Dudhsagar is Sonauli. Current timetables should be consulted, as alterations may be made to facilitate connections at Margao with the new Konkan railway service.

It seems unlikely, however, that timekeeping will prove any more reliable than in the past, and passengers must be prepared for long delays — take a good book (preferably this one) to while away the time. A packed lunch is also recommended, as little food of any quality is available in the area; cold drinks, however, are provided by vendors at the waterfalls.

For many, this will be their only train journey in India and, unless new carriages are employed, its spartan nature, even in first-class compartments, will be a surprise. Fortunately, the scenery for much of the route, particularly throughout Sanguem, is so beautiful that most will hardly notice any discomfort. Windows are kept small in Indian trains for protection against the sun and monsoon rain. Although it may appear so, the presence of horizontal bars across the windows does not imply that the train was once used for transporting prisoners; their purpose is evidently to deflect any missiles which might be hurled by youngsters having a 'lark' beside the track.

The cascades

There are two principal cascades at Dudhsagar, their sudden appearance on the right-hand side as the train exits from a tunnel always creating astonishment. On descending to the track, it will become apparent that the bridge on which the train stands bisects the face of the falls on its 600m (2,000ft) descent, via the pools, to the valley below.

When the cascade is at its most spectacular, there will be a great amount of spray (another reason for taking a towel) and care should be observed. The white foam created as the cascades reach the pools led to the name Dudhsagar, meaning, in Konkani, 'sea of milk'. Steps descend from the track directly to the first pool a short distance below.

From the opposite side of the railway line an esplanade provides views down to the distant, larger pool, where swimming is possible. This may only be reached by walking back along the railway track through the tunnel from which the train has just emerged and, at its end, following the downhill path, right.

The steep return journey is very exhausting, and visitors should be certain that they are in fit condition to make it without too much stress, particularly during the hot season. It must be said, however, that unless the descent is made, there is little more to do to while away the time before the next return train arrives.

Views of the Dudhsagar waterfalls from the lower pool are more comprehensive, and it is a delight to swim in the cool water. Some younger European visitors who have neglected to bring a costume swim in the nude rather than miss the treat; there are no officials to object, and those who might be offended are warned.

Bhagwan Mahaveer Wildlife Sanctuary

Kulem railway station lies only two miles south of **Molem** village, which stands on the edge of the Bhagwan Mahaveer Wildlife Sanctuary. It should not take long to locate some form of transport in Kulem village; several inhabitants will usually be happy to take visitors on their motorbikes to the sanctuary and Tambdi Surla Temple. Those with a car will drive direct to Molem along the main road from Ponda, avoiding Kulem until they wish to proceed by train to Dudhsagar.

It is possible to spend the night within the sanctuary in bungalows operated by the Goa Tourist Department Corporation, and this is the only way to have much chance of seeing the more spectacular animals; ensure to check the situation in advance, as accommodation is very limited. At the time of writing, food is provided

and treks by four-wheel drive vehicles operate early morning and late evening.

The sanctuary covers more than 200sq km (77sq miles) of land — some of it flat, where a few tigers have been seen, some of it upland, where the more numerous black panther roams. Here, as elsewhere in India, constant vigilance is needed to guard the big cats from gun-wielding poachers.

Many varieties of deer and herds of massive bison are here in abundance, as are the chattering monkeys. Elephants, rare in Goa, may also be seen. Walks have been laid out and, even if few animals are glimpsed, the birdlife and undulating landscape are a constant delight. In the direction of Molem lies "Devil's Canyon", where crocodiles may be seen basking on the river banks.

The Shri Mahadeva Temple

The unique Shri Mahadeva Temple at **Tambdi Surla** may be reached from Kulem station via Molem, but a slightly more direct route for those with private transport is followed by taking the left turn off the road from Ponda, just before the village of Darbandora is reached. This road passes Sancordem, and it is then necessary to take another left turn 3 km (2 miles) further on (immediately following the left turn to Surla village). The temple nestles below the mountains, dramatically appearing without warning in a forest clearing.

The Kadambas ruled Goa from the tenth to the fourteenth

century, and the high quality of their architecture was renowned; this temple, believed to have been erected in the thirteenth century, and the only important survival from that period, gives a tantalising hint of the splendours that have been lost. **In its subtle chunkiness, Tambdi Surla evokes Khmer temples in Thailand and Cambodia, and American Indian temples in Mexico and Guatemala.** However, it should be borne in mind that the *shikara* tower has been truncated and its finial lost; originally, therefore, the temple would have had a more vertical emphasis.

To The Shri Mahadeva Temple...

A romantically isolated position, a balance of strength and delicacy and superb craftsmanship, all these combine to produce the most thrilling building in Goa, which should not be missed by any lover of architecture. Most visitors will have learned in advance that the temple is small, but its exquisite proportions give it a gem-like quality, which makes dimensions irrelevant.

The many other Kadamba temples were destroyed by the Muslims, long before the arrival of the Portuguese, and Tambdi Surla's can only have survived because of its remoteness. There are no traces of ancient towns or villages nearby, which indicates that the site had some religious significance for the Kadambas; the large stones in the compound do not come from the existing structure, and suggest that other temples may have stood nearby.

The black basalt, of which the temple is entirely built, was favoured by the Kadambas, who presumably had discovered that detail carved on soft laterite would fade away in no time. Unfortunately for them, only laterite was available locally, and lengthy, arduous journeys, possibly through the mountains, would have been needed to obtain a hard stone; comparisons with the situation at Stonehenge in England come to mind. It seems that the Kadamba builders distrusted the weathering properties of mortar, as the temple has been erected using dry construction methods; this would have been a further reason for their preference for basalt, its weight being far greater than that of laterite.

The building rests on a three-stringed plinth, from which pilasters rise to provide the only vertical detailing of importance to the exterior of the sanctuary and its vestibule. They are met by a series of cornices, two of which are boldly dentilated. Truncated though it may be, the gently tapering *shikara* tower is still magnificent. Bas-relief tablets on three of its sides depict the Hindu trinity, with their consorts above;

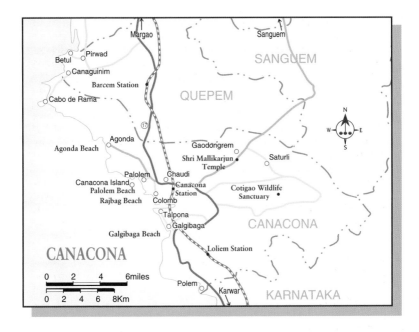

from the south side: Brahma, Shiva and Vishnu.

There is no entrance hall, and the *mandapa* can be approached directly from its three sides, the low walls of which are decorated with bands of lozenges and rosettes, their carving still crisp. The perimeter columns are simply designed, but the four pillars of the central bay appear to comprise many tiers: they are each, in fact, carved from single blocks of stone. At the base of the north-east column, an elephant is depicted trampling a horse, possibly an allegorical reference to Hindu victories over foreign invaders, as there seems to be no religious significance.

The ceiling of the *mandapa* is deeply carved with lotus flowers, its central panel being exceptionally fine. Four wall niches accommodate small figures of the serpent gods (Naga); the surrounds of the niches include a depiction of the temple's *shikara* tower, with its finial, as it appeared before it was truncated. The side walls of the *mandapa* are fitted with sloping, stone seat backs. A headless Nandi bull denotes that the temple is dedicated to Shiva.

Those who have seen the ruined doorway to Adil Shah's palace in Old Goa may note the resemblance between its fragment of lattice-work and that of the screen around the entrance to the tiny vestibule, the only complete example in Goa to survive. Some believe that this ancient Hindu feature inspired the screens developed by the Moghuls to hide their womenfolk, in purda, from public view. The rather squat Mahadeva *lingam* of Shiva stands on a large pedestal.

Canacona

In spite of boasting Goa's most idyllic beaches, Canacona *taluka*'s remoteness and lack of facilities had, until recently, preserved it from tourist development. Only the most intrepid made the long journey to Chaudi to search out accommodation in the nearby coastal village of Palolem. This meant that those wishing to escape the crowds and experience Goa's coatline as it once was — a succession of golden beaches entirely the preserve of fishermen and playful youngsters — could still do so, providing they accepted very basic accommodation and limited menus.

In 1998, however, the **Konkan Railway** at last opened, Canacona Station, just outside Chaudi, being provided with fast trains to the rest of Goa and onward to Bombay and Kerala. Change seems inevitable; and even before the railway opened, day trips by boat from the north to visit "Paradise Beach" at Palolem, combined with illegal beach shacks and accommodation were changing the virgin nature of the state.

Fortunately, most of the shacks have been removed by the authorities and a breathing space has been created. Nothing however can be done about the disfiguring graffitti painted on the great rocks around Palolem beach, most of it promoting the names of now extinct beach restaurants. In spite of some commercialisation however, Canacona remains idyllic, it is also very cheap, and, like the northern tip of Goa, popular with long-stay visitors. Only Kerala state's beaches in southern India can match its low prices, but there, alcoholic beverages are much dearer, due to the tax situation. Not only youthful back-packers are Canacona enthusiasts, which is hardly surprising as it has been calculated that by staying at home through the winter months, an average western visitor's bill for fuel, transport, warm clothing, water, insurance and the telephone, would match his total expenditure in Canacona for the same period.

One hopeful factor is that Canacona's villagers, almost unanimously, want to protect their simple way of life and, although welcoming visitors, prefer not to be swamped by them. It seems likely that they will examine all planning applications meticulously, and no more temporary or permanent buildings are likely to intrude on the palm-fringed shores.

Chaudi

Chaudi, the *taluka*'s chief 'town' is, in reality, little more than a village. There is one simple restaurant, a small fruit, vegetable and fish market and that is all.

At present, Canacona's visitors must travel to Margao in order to change traveller's cheques, and it is advisable, therefore, that all should arrive with a good supply of rupees, sterling notes or dollar bills. Although Canaconans are not untrustworthy, holidaymakers are advised to deposit bank notes with the owner of their accommodation — just in case.

There is a regular bus service from Chaudi to Margao, and also, now that the Konkan line has opened, a train service, which is much quicker, as there is only one scheduled stop (Bali) between the two stations. A few buses also continue from Chaudi to Palolem, but taxis, auto-rickshaws and motorbikes are always plentiful.

Palolem

A first sight of Palolem's beach always takes the breath away. It is undoubtedly Goa's most idyllic; soft golden sand lines a curving bay, almost one mile long, with steep headlands at both ends. To the right is tiny Canacona Island, which is linked with the rocky promontory by a natural causeway at low tide. Below the same headland, a fordable freshwater stream meanders down from the heights of the Western Ghat mountains to meet the sea.

The beach is relatively narrow and, at times, the coconut palms march down almost to the water's edge in approved tropical-beach style. A handful of thatched bars, most of which offer food, nestle beneath the palm trees.

Palolem village lies a hundred metres from the beach, to which it is connected by a short street. Most of the buildings straddle the Chaudi road, but some houses have been erected amid the palm trees between the road and the beach.

In spite of increased tourism, Palolem's accommodation and food leave much to be desired. Nearest the beach, off the approach road to it, **Palolem Beach**

'Piggy toilets'

One word of warning. Those of a squeamish nature should bear in mind that most villagers keep pigs, and Goan pigs eat absolutely anything. Many of the toilets in Canacona are not directly connected to a sewage pipe, but are raised on stilts above a cess pit; they are grimly referred to by visitors as 'piggy toilets', for reasons that need not be dwelt on here. In view of this, some may wish to inspect the toilet facilities before agreeing terms for a room in family accommodation.

Resort (☎ 643054) comprises tents (unlockable) with communal shower/toilet blocks. Its restaurant serves reasonable food, but waiting can be interminable. On the same road the new Cupid Castle (no telephone) offers spartan rooms — but with en-suite shower/wc, a rarity in Palolem.

Of the family accommodation, **Rosy's (or D'Mella Tourist Home,** ☎ 643057), on the Chaudi road, is still the best, particularly as rooms with shower/wc have been added recently. Most Palolem tourists are western youngsters and junk food therefore predominates. The best restuarant is the extremely friendly **Sun & Moon,** opposite Rosy's, but arrive very early or very late to avoid long delays as it is very popular.

The headlands

Both Palolem headlands may be scrambled over without too much difficulty, to examine the rock pools and caves, and to visit Canacona Island, the rather grandly named islet which can be reached at low tide. One might well be joined by a tribe of scampering monkeys, particularly in the evening; they will not pause for conversation and usually bare their teeth when approached too closely. Holidaymakers given to nudism particularly favour the beach at this point.

There is no northbound path, but, at the southern extremity of the beach, a delightful track leads through palm trees behind the headland, to reveal a succession of small, sandy bays, each delineated by fingers of rock pointing seaward.

The fishing village of **Colomb,** soon reached, adds to the picturesque quality of the scene, which almost appears too good to be true — as if an exhibition designer had been involved in its layout. Just behind Colomb Beach lies the family run Hotel Sea View (☎ 643110); the only accommodation in this area. Its staff are most friendly and helpful. Serving the best food in the Palolem region, the **Candlelight Beach Restaurant** on Colomb Beach should not be missed — assuming the authorities have continued to permit it to stay.

Rajbag Beach

By keeping to the shore, the beautiful uninhabited beach of Rajbag is reached. At times this will be cut off, as a stream, the Rajbag River, gets delusions of grandeur at high tide; keep an eye on it to avoid making a long detour for the return journey. **Molyma,** a small, modern hotel has recently been constructed some distance behind the beach, however, in spite of its modernity, it cannot be classed as tourist standard. Nevertheless, this is certainly far superior to to any other accommodation in Canacona, and those

Opposite: The Dudhasagar Waterfalls, which drop a total of 2,000ft (600m), the highest in India

with their own transport might be tempted to stay for at least a few nights; there are rumours of upgrading and a hotel-run beach bar. An enormous luxury hotel is planned for Rajbag Beach to be operated by an international chain. One can only guess what effect it will have on the region, and much depends on planning regulations being strictly enforced.

Galgibaga Beach

The wide inlet of the River Talpona marks an end to this marine promenade, surely India's most appealing, but beyond lies Galgibaga Beach — yet another stretch of sand, but completely different in character. This definitely involves transport, preferably a motorbike, as a wide detour must be made to reach it from Palolem. The main road curves eastward from Chaudi, crossing the River Talpona. A right turn then leads uphill, soon dramatically revealing, far below, the winding river approaching its inlet.

Galgibaga village lies to the south and is approached by a left turn followed by a right turn. In spite of its remoteness, Galgibaga appears to be a popular place to live, as its fine houses, neat gardens and paths have little of the Third World about them.

Cotigao Wildlife Sanctuary

Bisected by the River Talpona, the **Wildlife Sanctuary** at Cotigao, the third to be established in Goa, lies to the east of the curving road between Palolem and Galgibaga. This sanctuary covers around 100sq km (40sq miles)

Galgibaga Beach

The beach at Galgibaga stretches along the southern edge of a narrow isthmus, which separates the sea from the River Galgibaga; there is, therefore, water on both sides. A big surprise is that Canacona's ubiquitous palm trees have been replaced by delicately fronded casuarina trees, their regularity indicating that they have been planted by man. No other beach in Goa looks like Gaglibaga's, nor does any other match its solitude.

At the river-end of the beach, rocks form a protective barrier against the famous Goan swell, and bathers can splash about happily in a non-turbulent sea. Food can often be obtained from the village bar, but it is safer to place an order on arrival. Otherwise, take a picnic lunch.

and is encircled by a minor road. Boards at the entrances indicate the presence of exotic species, but only rarely will any of them make an appearance. Locals cynically suggest that most of the animals retreated to the hills as soon as the sanctuary was announced. However, monkeys, deer and birdlife are compensations. As yet, there is nowhere to lodge within the sanctuary.

The village of **Gaodongrem** is reached from a road which runs northward from the Cotigao Sanctuary, via Saturli. Here is situated the **Shri Mallikarjun Temple**. Few Hindu temples of interest exist in Canacona and, while not approaching the grandeur of those of Ponda, this example, nestling in its valley, is the finest in the *taluka*.

Cabo de Rama Fort

A more important road returns from Gaodongrem to the main Chaudi road. From Palolem, a left turn before Chaudi is reached leads eventually to the dramatic site of Cabo de Rama Fort, Goa's most southerly example.

Little of structural interest remains of the fortification, and the chief reasons for a visit are the splendid marine views gained from the wild, rocky promontory on which it was built. The Portuguese took possession of the fort in 1763, but abandoned it in the 1830s, deciding that its military usefulness was at an end.

Overlooking a dry moat, the main entrance is now dilapidated, but the small chapel inside this still functions. The majority of the structural remains are of former barracks. From the western edge of the promontory, views stretch southward to Goa's last headland before Karnataka state, bulging out beyond Galgibaga; northward, the great length of Colva Beach fades into the Mormugao hills.

Between Palolem and Cabo de Rama lies yet another fine beach, fronting the village of **Agonda**. This comprises a straight, mile-long stretch of sand. It is, however, backed by rather flat terrain, and therefore lacks the picturesque quality typical of other Canacona beaches.

Betul

The road northward soon passes through Canaquinim, just in Quepem *taluka*, and a left turn descends to the villages of Pirwad and Betul. Betul is a pleasant fishing settlement, its houses built, untypically, right on the waters edge. Boats are needed to reach Betul Beach.

Polem Beach

Just before Goa merges into Karnataka, one more beach should be mentioned — at Polem — the most remote of them all. The curving sandy bay is very pretty, but facilities are extremely limited. From time to time, accommodation is erected on the beach by "Paradise Found". A ten minute walk from the Chaudi road through paddyfields leads to the beach. Most will be content with a half day visit.

7 Hampi

Hampi (Vijayanagar)

Visitors to Goa are well-placed to visit what has been described as 'virtually a vast open-air museum of Hindu monuments' — the ruined city of Vijayanagar, now known as Hampi. Understandably, western visitors find Hindhu architecture more exotic than Christian or Muslim, particularly the Dravidian temples of the south, with their towering gopura entrances, profuse, often exquisite, carving and formidable idols.

Hampi covers an area of around nine square miles, much of the hilly site being strewn with huge boulders. It can be reached from Panaji by car in seven hours, and the highlights may be seen by those with a private vehicle in around the same amount of time; a minimum of two days should therefore be allocated to the excursion. Most will find the inexpensive services of a knowledgeable guide to be indispensible.

How to get to Hampi

Until the conversion of the metre gauge railway is completed, Hampi can only be reached from Goa by road via the towns of Dharwad, Hubli, Gadag Betgeri, Koppal and Hospet, all in the state of Karnataka. The seven hour car journey is neither comfortable, due to the poor state of the road once Karnataka has been reached, nor is it particularly attractive, apart from the short stretch around the state border, where the Western Ghat mountains are crossed — the remainder is flat, much of it cotton plantation land.

Air-conditioned night buses run from Goa to Hampi in around eight hours, but don't expect much sleep or comfort.

When to go

Temperatures away from the coast in south India are much more extreme, March and April, for example, registering afternoon temperatures of more than 40°C. If travelling to Hampi in these months an air-conditioned car is virtually essential (even at double the usual kilometre hire rate).

Where to stay

Hospet (13km from Hampi)

The **Malligi Tourist Home** (☎ 8101) is by far the best place to stay in the Hampi area, even though its bedrooms' air-con-

ditioning units tend to reverberate — insist on a room test. An adjacent swimming pool is a great boon and the restaurant serves first rate food. At no matter what time check-in is made, guests are generously permitted a 24-hour stay. Organised tours and individual guides can be booked at reception.

Kamalapuram Village

The new Hotel Mayura Bhavaneshwari (☎ 5374), somewhat cheaper, is highly recommended: vegetarian and non-vegetarian food is provided, but there is no bedroom air-conditioning (even of the noisy type) and, of course, no pool. A great advantage is the hotel's immediate proximity to Hampi.

Vijayanagar's foundation

Vijayanagar was founded around 1336 by two brothers, Bukka and Harihara, following the collapse of the Hoysala dynasty. Its site was protected on three sides by ridges and on the fourth by the Tungabhadra River, which flows through a rocky gorge to the north. The plentiful supply of boulders was probably considered an advantage and their application in building the walls remains apparent.

A Great Empire

At its peak in the early 16th century, the Vijayanagar Empire incorporated most of south India, Krishna Raja, 1509-29, being regarded as its most influential leader. Arts and crafts were

Opposite: Spice seller in Hampi Bazaar

promoted and new technology developed. Although most citizens were Hindu, they followed various sects, and Muslims and Jains were permitted to worship in their mosques and temples without hindrance. As in medieval Europe, craftsmen and merchants formed guilds; textiles, iron ore and agricultural produce providing the basis of the empire's economic strength.

Muslim Conquest

In 1565, Muslim sultanates banded together to challenge the Vijayanagars, who they defeated at the seminal battle of Talikota. Although the ruler and his court survived, they made no attempt to defend the city of Vijayanagar, which was comprehensively sacked and burned. However the empire continued to rule much of the south for another century, before succumbing to another Muslim assault. Only a brief period of time elapsed before villagers moved in to take over what remained of the old city's bazaar to the north-west, which they called Hampi, a derivative of a local name for Shiva.

Hampi Village

On Hemakuta Hill, overlooking the village, the series of plain granite temples, with stepped shikara towers, are believed to date from the tenth century, ie 400 years before the Vijayanagars. Noteworthy are the two enormous Ganesh, elephant-headed god monoliths, respectively 10 and 18 feet high.

In the village, the brilliant colours of the Karnataka saris worn by the ladies will immediately impress those visitors who have become used to the less exotic dress worn by Goans. An even greater surprise to them will be the abundance of wild langur monkeys, a rare sight in Goa.

The great **Virupaksha Temple**, which dominates **Hampi bazaar**, is

The ruined city

Vijayanagar's sacred area, where major temples have survived in reasonable condition, skirts the south bank of the river, beginning just outside Hampi Bazaar. It is separated from the secular core of the city to the south by canals, which still irrigate a shallow valley. In spite of its natural defences, the city was fortified by a series of stone walls, laid out in concentric circles radiating from the royal enclosure. Visitors are usually directed to six distinct areas highlighted respectively by: Hampi Village, The Sule Bazaar, The Royal Enclosure, The Vittal Temple, Kamalapuram Village and the Narasimha Colossus.

the only building in Hampi that continues to function as a place of worship. On the north side, it is entered from a 52m (165ft) high gopuram. Noteworthy amongst much fine craftsmanship are the Shiva paintings on the ceiling and the animal carving on the pillars of the mandapam hall. Shrines carved in the Chalyuka and Hoysala periods are some of Hampi's oldest monuments.

A dramatic footpath between immense boulders follows the river northwards.

Sule Bazaar

Now deserted, this stretch of stone-built shop units is alleged to have been the city's red-light district, beckoning ladies presumably once leaning against the pillars. At the far end, the **Achyutara Temple** is neglected by most tourists in spite of its splendid carving. From this temple, a footpath leads southward to the **Royal Enclosure** (2kms) or, alternatively, another path continues northward to the **Vittal Temple**. Usually, however, those with a vehicle will be driven to the Royal Enclosure, via Hampi Village, and then to the Vittala Temple. On route are seen the **Sister Stones**, two enormous boulders leaning against each other.

Royal Enclosure

Extremely well-preserved are the **Elephant Stables**, each of the eleven stalls being flanked by two-storey domed pavilions. To the west lies the **Zenana** (women's quarter), from which

survives the famous **Lotus Mahal**; its name derives from a lotus bud carved in the ceiling. Domed pavilions squeezed together in a cicle result in a palace with an endearing, albeit dumpy, appearance

The **Hazara Rama**, further south, is believed to have been the chapel royal. Enclosing walls are carved with bands of outstanding friezes depicting elephants, horse training, troops, and dancing girls. Around the walls of the temple are carved scenes from the Ramayana. Internally, the pillars of the mandapam hall exhibit well-preserved bas-reliefs illustrating the avatars of Vishnu.

To the west, the so-called **Underground Temple** gained its name because it was buried by rubble during the despoilation of the city: excavation continues. Only the basements and wall fragments of the three marble **palaces** recorded by 16th century visitors have survived.

Ruinous but still charming is the **Queen's Bath**, to the south. The vaulted ceiling of its corridor is carved with flowers, and the balconies exhibit delightful filigree work. A strong Islamic influence is apparant throughout.

The road northward towards the Vittala Temple passes through the picturesque **Talari Katta Gate** before a left branch is taken.

Vittala Temple

This temple, dedicated to Vishnu, is one of the three in south India that have been awarded **World Heritage status**. The complex, begun in 1521, was never completed for worship; however, it is regarded as the finest example of Vijayanagar art.

Within the enclosing wall are three separate temples with gopura towers, but the largest is undoubtedly the finest. Particularly impressive is the carving of the columns, depicting mounted yali (mythical lions), some of which are supported by elephants. The external columns emit a musical note when tapped, but visitors are requested not to test this out to avoid eventual damage. Unsightly blocks of concrete, recently erected beside some of the columns for structural reasons, somewhat spoil the overall effect, and it must be hoped that a more aesthetically pleasing solution to the problem will eventually be found. A carved stone rath (chariot) stands before the temple; apparently, its wheels once turned.

Resembling a gateway, the **King's Balance** lies to the south of the complex. On his birthday, the king would be weighed against gold, coins or grain which would then be distributed amongst the needy.

Overlooking the river, the columns of the **Purandara Dasara** (guesthouse) are strangely carved with female monkeys and dwarfs. Purandara was a contemporary musician of distinction. Across the river can be seen the remains of the bridge that once provided a link between both banks.

Kamalapuram Village

The village, which provides a second road entry point to Hampi, is primarily of interest for those staying in its hotel or visiting its museum. The museum (open 10am to 5pm) exhibits Vijayanagar exhibits discovered at Hampi, and includes exquisite sculptures and coinage. A model of Hampi is displayed outside.

On returning to Hampi village, most will stop on route to examine the last group of important monuments.

Narasimha Colossus

Erected in 1528, the colossal monolithic figure of Narasimha (or Narasingh), an avatar of Vishnu, glares out at visitors disturbingly from its simple granite-block enclosure. Even though the arms have been demolished, this 6.7m (22ft) high figure, with bulbous eyes and a greedy mouth, is the most powerful of Hampi's idols. Within the adjacent **Badavi Temple** stands an unusually large Siva lingam.

Further north, a **Krishna Temple** complex of 1513 is approached via an inscribed gopuram. Carving throughout is noteworthy.

Opposite: —
Left: Frizes of exquisite bas-reliefs are distinctive feature of Vijayanagar temples
Right: The terrifying Narasimha Colossus is the most impressive of Hampi's shrines
Below: The famous stone carriage (rath) within the Vittala Temple complex

ACCOMMODATION

Goa offers a wide range of visitor accommodation, from basic rooms in villagers' homes to luxury resort hotels with all the expected facilities. A grading system is operated, ranging from one to five stars. All rooms in a star-rated establishment will be provided with en-suite showers and toilets, telephones and televisions. A high percentage of visitors to Goa will have pre-booked their accommodation. If not, it is best to select the resort area and ask advice from a taxi driver or at the beach bars. For those who wish to stay near the more intimate beaches north of Baga, or in Canacona *taluka*, there is little star-rated accommodation available.

During the high season of December and January, prices are slightly higher in all establishments, but considerably higher in the upper-grade hotels. At this time, also, accommodation may be difficult to find in the most popular areas. Individual hotels and boarding houses are described in some detail in the brochures of tour operators that specialize in Goa.

CLIMATE

The south-west monsoon usually hits Goa during the first week in June, petering out in September. Rains are very heavy, particularly in July and August, when few holidaymakers will wish to visit. From mid-September to the end of May, rainfall is light, and a minimum of seven hours sunshine per day can be expected. April and May are definitely hot. Only when there is cloud cover, a rare event, does the humidity become uncomfortable. At night, in January, the temperature can drop to 68°F, which the Goans regard as a freeze-up. Tourists, however, will find that a light pullover will more than suffice. Sea temperatures vary little throughout the year, and the water is always slightly refreshing, rather like the Mediterranean in early summer; the 'hot bath' warmth of South-East Asian seas will not be found. Strong winds are rare throughout the dry season.

CURRENCY REGULATIONS

A maximum of 250 rupees (less than £5 at current rates) may be brought into or taken out of the country. In theory, amounts of foreign currency or travellers cheques in excess of US$1,000 should be declared on arrival in India, but in practice, this appears to be unnecessary. Visitors staying more than 90 days have to apply for an income tax exemption certificate; to obtain

this, currency exchange forms must be produced
(see also: **Money**).

CUSTOMS REGULATIONS

One bottle of spirits and 200 cigarettes may be brought into
India. Valuable items, such as cameras, transistors, etc may
have to be entered in a Tourist Baggage Re-Export form to
ensure that they will not be re-sold in India, where they are
extremely expensive. The form and the items concerned must
be shown on departure.

ELECTRICITY

Throughout Goa, voltage is 230-240 AC. All sockets take
continental plugs and most take UK two-point plugs, but not
always; bring a continental adaptor. Men should also take wet
razors (and blades) in case of power cuts. Large hotels have
their own generators, otherwise power cuts can occur at any
time. However, times of cuts are published and rarely last more
than half an hour.

HEALTH

Currently, it is recommended that visitors to India are injected
against typhoid, paratyphoid, tetanus, polio and hepatitis A.
During the dry season, few mosquitoes are seen in Goa's
coastal regions, and malaria is rare, nevertheless, many may
wish to take precautions. Seek advice on the current situation
some weeks before leaving from a pharmacy or a general
practitioner. Drugs such as chloroquine and proquanil offer 70
per cent protection, but take insect repellent — and use it. Also
enquire about qinhaosu, an ancient Chinese remedy now being
researched. If particularly worried about health dangers,
specialist hospitals will give detailed advice; in the UK contact
the Hospital for Tropical Diseases Travel Clinic
☎ 0171 637 9899.

Rabies is common throughout India, and visitors are
recommended not to pat dogs or hand-feed monkeys. If bitten,
seek medical advice immediately.

Most stomach upsets in Goa are caused by an excess of
chillis, and are quickly disposed of by proprietary medicines
such as Immodium. It is best that these are brought by the
visitor so that action can be taken as soon as discomfort is
experienced. Tap water should be rigorously avoided outside
the luxury hotels, as should any fresh fruit and salad vegetables
that may have been rinsed in it. Check with the establishment

(cont'd on page 152)

Festivals

Goan festivals are many, and most of them are held on dates which vary each year, according to religious calendars. Ascertain precise dates on arrival in Goa.

Name of Festival	Venue
January	
Feast of Three Kings (6 January)	Cansaulim (Mormugao)
	Chandor (Salcete)
	Reis Magos (Bardez)
Jatra at Shri Shantadurga Temple Makar Sankranti	Fatorpa (Quepem)
Jatra at Shri Bogdgeshwar Temple	Mapusa (Bardez)
Jatra at Shri Devkikrishna Ravalnath Temple	Marcela (Ponda)
February	
Feast of Our Lady of Candelaria (2 February)	Pomburpa (Bardez)
Vasant Panchami Jatra at Shri Shantadurga Temple	Queula (Ponda)
Jatra at Shri Ajoba Temple	Querim (Pernem)
Hatra at Shri Manguesh Temple	Priol (Ponda)
Jatra at Shri Mahalsa Temple	Mardol (Ponda)
Utsav at Shri Mahalaxmi Temple	Amone (Bicholim)
Intruz 3 day carnival	Panaji
March	
Mahashivratri Jatras	Siroda (Ponda)
	Ramnath (Ponda)
	Sanguem
Jatra	Fatorpa (Quepem)
Jatra (Gulal) at Shri Damodar Temple	Zambaulim (Sanguem)
April	
Gudi Padva Jatra at Shri Kalikadevi	
Kansarpa (Bicholim) Temple Ramzan -Id	
Procession of All Saints (Monday following Palm Sunday)	Goa Velha (Tiswadi)

Ramnavami Jatra	Partagal Math (Canacona)
Shri Mahavir Jayanti	Borim (Ponda)
Hanuman Jayanti Jatras	Nagesh (Ponda)
	Sanquelim (Bicholim)
	Chandranath (Salcete)
	Marutigadh-Kakoda (Quepem)

May

Feast of Our Lady of Miracles (16 days after Good Friday)	Mapusa (Bardez)
Jatra (fire-walking) at Shri Lairai Temple	Sirigao (Bicholim)
Jatra at Shri Narasimha Temple	Velinga (Ponda)

October

Kojagiri Poornima Dussehra Mahotsava	Pernem
Fama de Menino Jesus (3rd Sunday in October)	Colva (Salcete)

November

Mandrem Saptah	Mandrem (Pernem)
Dindi at Vithal Temple	Margao
Jatra	Borim (Ponda)
Jatra at Shri Naguesh Temple	Nagesh (Ponda)
Jatra at Marcaim	Marcaim (Ponda)
Feast of Our Lady of the Rosary	Velim (Salcete)
Jatra at Amone	Amone (Bicholim)
Candepar	(Ponda)
Jatra at Shri Vandevi Temple	Mulgaon (Bicholim)
Banastari	(Ponda)
Jatra at Shri Anant Temple	Savoi-Verem (Ponda)
Utsav at Shri Santeri Temple	Mapusa (Bardez)

December

Feast of St Francis Xavier	Old Goa
Jatra at Shri Vijayadurga Temple	Querim (Ponda)
Feast of Our Lady of Immaculate Conception	Panaji
Datta Jayanti, Utsav at Shri Datta Mandir Temple	Sanquelim (Bicholim)

to ensure that the water that they provide has been purified. Ice made from unpurified tap water can also be dangerous, as the freezing process does not kill the microbes which cause the problems. Indians have developed immunity to them and can drink most water without fear. Bottled mineral water is readily available in tourist areas, but should be bought in advance if travelling elsewhere. Ensure that the water is sealed, or it may have been refilled with tap water. It is recommended that teeth are brushed in purified or mineral water whenever possible. Purification tablets should be brought for use in an emergency.

While Goan pharmacies and doctors in the main towns are generally most efficient, it is preferable that any medical supplies that might be required are brought by visitors. Hospitals exist in Panaji, Margao, Mapusa and Vasco de Gama.

If worrying symptoms develop on returning home, contact a specialist hospital immediately, eg in the UK the Hospital for Tropical Diseases, 4 St Pancras Way, London NW1 0PE ☎ 0171 387 4411. Help is also available regionally in Birmingham, Liverpool and Glasgow.

MAPS

An excellent map of Goa, scale 1:160,000 is provided by TT Maps and Publications (Madras) for the Goa Department of Tourism. Copies are available at Dabolim Airport from Car Rental companies; this will be the most convenient source for most visitors. For those travelling to other parts of India, the Nelles Sectional series, scale 1:1500,000, is highly recommended.

MONEY

The Indian currency is the rupee, which is divided into 100 paise (pronounced pies). Formerly, the rupee was also divided into sixteen annas, but the anna is no longer in use. American dollars and sterling are the simplest currencies to exchange in India, whether they be in note or travellers cheque form. Many hotels in Goa will change money for their guests, and the rate given is now very little less than that obtainable from banks. Indian banks should be avoided whenever possible, as the infamous red tape and form-filling involved means that a simple transaction may take several hours. Banking hours are: Monday to Friday 10am-2pm, Saturday 10am-12noon. Always insist on plenty of low-value notes, as no-one ever has any change. Never accept torn or damaged notes, because Indians are loth to take them. Ensure that currency exchange forms are given for each transaction, and keep them, for exchanging any remaining rupees when leaving India, or for obtaining a tax clearance certificate if staying more than ninety days. It is best to pay a travel agent to obtain this, in order to avoid the tiresome official procedure: involving a solicitor, a local Income Tax office, a main Income Tax office, and a return to visit the latter three days later. Most banks in small towns throughout Goa will not be able to change travellers cheques — this applies to the entire *taluka* of Canacona. The most welcome travellers cheques in India are those issued by American Express and Thomas Cook, both in dollars.

PACKING

As no heavy clothes will be needed in Goa, and hotels provide a fast, reliable laundry service, it is unnecessary to pack a large amount of clothing. The standard allowance permitted by most tour operators is 20kg plus hand baggage. Toiletries, a simple medical kit and camera film (particularly for colour slides) should be brought, but all clothing is very much cheaper throughout India, much of it of excellent quality, particularly in the large towns. Jackets and trousers, for example, can be made to measure in a couple of days, so leave plenty of room or bring items that can be discarded.

Long-life batteries can be hard to find, as can deodorants, outside the large cities. If a cocktail before a meal is appreciated, a hip-flask, filled from a duty free bottle, is recommended. Unless staying at a top class hotel, do not be surprised if there is no plug for the sink in the bathroom; take an adaptable rubber plug. Thick socks can also come in useful if temples are being visited — shoes must always be removed and the stone can be very hot. For the beach, sandals although generally useful, let in the burning hot sand and canvas shoes which can be adjusted easily with velcro are better. Those intending to send letters should take envelopes or a glue stick as Indian envelopes have no adhesive strip.

PASSPORTS

All visitors to India must have a passport, valid for six months after their return date. Holders of Indian passports are not permitted to travel to India on chartered flights, which virtually rules out most package tours to Goa for them. A visa for India is required by all visitors.

POLICE

If police assistance is urgently required, telephone 100 43400, however, it is initially preferable to seek advice from a hotel.

POSTAGE

Stamps may be purchased at hotels or post offices, but the latter always involve long, slow-moving queues. The postal service is remarkably quick, efficient and honest. Mail sent home should arrive in one week. Never even think about sending a parcel out of India, the procedure demanded is a nightmare. Look with suspicion on offers by stores to post goods overseas; they may or may not arrive. This does not, of course, apply to state-run emporiums or shops sited within large hotels. Post offices are open Monday to Friday 10am-5pm and Saturday 10am-12noon.

TIME

Goa, like the rest of India, is 5¹/2 hours ahead of GMT.

TIPPING

Tipping (*backsheesh*) is widely practised in India, as in most Third-World countries. Only very small amounts are usually expected, so carry plenty of low-denomination notes and coins to give for minor services. It is usual for the service charge to be included in restaurant bills. If not, tip the waiter 10 per cent. Taxi drivers and auto-rickshaw operators will generally quote an inclusive price, but for good service, a small additional tip is appreciated.

TOURIST INFORMATION

Much information can be obtained from hotel reception staff and representatives of tour operators, many of whom make daily visits to the hotels. Tourist Information Centres which can supply information about Goa are situated at:
Dabolim Airport (☎ 2644); Panaji Inter-State Bus Terminus (☎ 5620); Margao, Tourist Hostel (☎ 22153); and Vasco da Gama, Tourist Hotel (☎ 2673). Information about other areas of India may be obtained from the Government of India Tourist Office, Communidade Building, Church Square, Panaji (☎ 3412).

GOVERNMENT OF INDIA TOURIST OFFICES:

UK
7 Cork Street, London
W1X 1PB
☎ (0171) 437 3677

USA
Suite 204, 3550 Wilshire
Boulevard, Los Angeles CA
90010
☎ (213) 380 8855
Suite 1808, 1270 Avenue of
the Americas, New York,
NY 10020
☎ (212) 586 4901/2/3

Canada
West Suite No 1003, 60 Bloor
Street, Toronto, Ontario M4W
3B8
☎ (416) 962 3787/88

Australia
Level 2, 210 Pitt Streert,
Sydney NSW 2000
☎ (9) 264 4855

TRAVEL

AIR
Only chartered aircraft fly direct to Goa's Dabolim airport from
abroad. Unless travelling with a tour operator or Air India,
therefore, the nearest airport to Goa for overseas visitors is
Bombay, an hour's flight away. At the time of writing, five
internal airlines operate between Bombay and Goa: Indian
Airlines, Modsluft and Jet Airways. In the UK, Savetime Travel
(☎ 0181 903 8777) will reserve Indian Airlines flights, while Jet
Airways flights can be booked from Jetair (UK) Ltd (☎ London
0181 970 1525 or Manchester 0161 228 1724).

Visitors travelling with tour operators will automatically be
met at the airport by buses to take them to their resort
accommodation. Many hotels, including some quite small
establishments, will also meet individual holidaymakers at the
airport. International return flights from India on scheduled (not
chartered) aircraft must be confirmed, usually one week in
advance of departure. Check the situation immediately on
arrival in India, as it can be almost impossible to contact
international airlines, apart from Air India, by telephone from
Goa.

Taxis are plentiful outside the airport, but those on low
budgets, who wish to travel southward by bus, are
recommended to make the 5km journey to Vasco da Gama bus
station, from where they will have a chance of getting a seat.
There is a bus service from the airport to Panaji (29km),
operated by Indian Airlines. When the new Konkan, north/
south Goa railway is fully operational, many will wish to be

taken direct to the nearest station, and continue by train — ask on arrival at the airport.

Telephone numbers in Panaji: Air India 22 4081, 22 5172; Indian Airlines 22 43826, 22 43831, 22 44067. It is imperative to remember that a departure from India tax of 300 rupees is levied at all Indian airports.

TRAIN

The Konkan railway line from Bombay to the Kerala border opened at last in 1988, but few trains were running. When finally operational, the service will link most tourist areas of Goa from north to south and, even more important, reduce the journey to Bombay to around eight hours. Trains should soon be running from Vasco de Gama eastward via Dudshagar Falls to Karnataka and connections for Hampi and Bangalore. All depends on completing the conversion of the existing metre gauge track to wide gauge — an extremely slow business. Check the current situation on arrival.

BUS

Just about every town and village of any size in Goa has a bus service of sorts, and all the coastal areas can be reached with ease. From Baga northward, however, it is necessary to travel inland to Mapusa, and then back again towards the sea, in order to reach the next coastal village northward; hired transport is a better bet.

TAXIS ETC

Vehicles hired in the manner of taxis come in four forms, these are, in descending order of cost: tourist taxis, black and yellow taxis, auto-rickshaws (virtually enclosed three-wheel motorbikes) and motorbikes. All have meters, but, on spotting a tourist, their drivers are often loth to use them 'meter no working'. For a longer distance it is essential to bargain.

CAR & MOTORBIKE HIRE

Budget and Hertz have branches in Goa, and there are a multitude of smaller organisations. Those non-resident in India may now hire self-drive cars, however, the supplement for including a driver is negligible. Motorbikes may be hired, but few directions are given, roads are not numbered and the routes are littered with unpredictable animals. Throughout India, driving is on the left. Those intending to hire a motor bike should bring an international driving licence, ensure that full insurance cover is obtained and bring a helmet. Note that bikes hired in Goa may not be taken to another state.

SHIPS

A catamaran service is operated by Damania Shipping daily in
season between Old Ferry Wharf, Bombay and Panaji Jetty,
Goa. The journey takes seven hours each way and reservations
may be made at Damania Shipping Offices. Upper-deck
bookings are slightly dearer than the air fare; lower-deck
bookings are slightly cheaper.

VISAS

All foreign passport holders need a visa to enter India. In the
case of the United Kingdom, this measure was introduced as a
tit-for-tat by Indira Gandhi, when the British government
decided to require Indians visiting the UK to obtain a visa,
thereby ensuring that they were not immigrating illegally.

It is advisable to make postal application for visas at least
two months in advance, although personal applicants are
usually able to collect their visas on the same day — after a
lengthy queue and then a wait. Tourist six-month visas should
specify multi-entry validity, if trips to Sri Lanka, the Maldives or
Nepal, for example are envisaged. Business visas are available
for a twelve-month period, but cannot be obtained on the same
day. The validity of the visa now commences on the date of
arrival in India. Would-be visitors to India without a valid
passport and visa will not be permitted to board the plane, nor
can any refunds be expected. Travel agents are able to advise
on the current procedure.

In the United Kingdom, visas must be obtained from the
following:

High Commision of India, India House, Aldwych, London WC2
B4NA (☎ 0171 240 2084)
Consulate General of India, 20 Augustus Street, Jewellery
Quarters, Hockley, Birmingham B18 6JL (☎ 0121 212 2782)
Consulate General of India, 6th Floor, Fleming House, 134
Rengrew Street, Glasgow, G3 75T (☎ 0141 331 0777)
In Eire: The Embassy of India, 6 Lesson Park, Dublin 6
(☎ 497 0843)

Three passport-size photographs are required. If a visa is
needed urgently, and personal application is difficult, passport
and visa courier services exist that will simplify and speed up
the process for a fee; a visa can generally be obtained in seven
working days by this means. One such organisation is **Thames
Consular**, 363 Chiswick High Road, London W4 4HS
(☎ 0181 995 2492).

Index

A

Agassaim 73
Albuquerque
    mansion 38
Anant Devasthan
    Temple 105
Anjuna Beach 37
Arambol Beach 40
Arch of the
    Viceroys 88
Archaeological
    Museum 86
Azad Maidan
    Square 66

B

Baga 48
Baga Beach 36
Benaulim 116
Betalbatim 113
Betim 45
Betul 141
Bhagwan
    Mahaveer
    Wildlife
    Sanctuary 133
Bicholim Taluka 54
Bondla Wildlife
    Sanctuary 109
Britona 46

C

Cabo de
    Rama Fort 141
Calangute 46
Calangute Beach 36

Canacona 136
Candepar 108
Candola 108
Caves of Lamgao 55
Chandor 125
Chandranath Hill 128
Chapora 38
Chaudi 137
Chorao Island 56
Church of Our Lady
    of the Mount 93
Church of Our Lady
    of The Rosary 92
Church of St
    Cajetan 89
Church of St
    Francis of
    Assisi 85
Coco Beach 44
Colomb 139
Colva 113
Colva Beach 112
Convent of
    St Monica 89
Cotigao Wildlife
    Sanctuary 140

D

Deshprabhu
    House 51
Divar Island 56
Dona Paula
    Beach 70
Dudhsagar
    Waterfalls 130

F

Fauna and Flora 21
Feast of Reis
    Magos 45
Fontainhas
    Quarter 68
Food and Drink 26
Fort Aguada 40

G

Galgibaga
    Beach 140
Gateway of the
    Palace of Adil
    Shah 88
Geography 20
Goa Velha 73
Gowapuri 71

H

Hampi 142
Harvalem caves 55
Hindu Temples of
    Ponda 95
History 12

J

Jua Island 57

K

Konkan Railway 156

L

Laterite Stone 21

M

Majorda Beach   113
Malpem   52
Mandrem Beach   38
Mapusa   49
Mauli Temple at
 Sarmalem   52
Menezes Braganza
 House   125
Minor Basilica of
 Bom Jesus   78
Miramar Beach   69
Miranda House   124
Moira   51
Morgim Beach   38
Mormugao   112
Municipal Garden   61
Music   24

N

Northern
 Beaches   35

O

Old Goa   74
Opa   109
Our Lady of the
 Snows   123

P

Palolem   137
Panaji   58
Parcem   53
Pernem town   51
Pilar Sominary   71

Pillory   92
Polem Beach   141

Q

Querim   52

R

Rachol Fort   123
Rachol
 Seminary   121
Rajbag Beach   139
Reis Magos
 church   44
Religions   22

S

Safa Shahouri
 Mosque   104
Saligao   48
Salvador Costa
 House   124
Sanguem   130
Sanquelim   55
Sao Thome
 Quarter   66
Se Cathedral   84
Secretariat   61
Shri Bhagavati
 Temple   52
Shri Damodar
 Temple   127
Shri Laxmi
 Narasimha
 Temple   100
Shri Mahadeva
 Tomplo   133

Shri Mahalaxmi
 Temple   101
Shri Mahalsa
 Temple   97
Shri Mangesh
 Temple   96
Shri Nagesh
 Temple   101
Shri Ramnath
 Temple   104
Shri Saptakoteshwar
 Temple   54
Shri Shantadurga
 Temple   102
Sinquerim Beach
 36
Souza Goncalves
 House   49
Sport   24
Statue of Abbé
 Faria   64

T

Talaulim   73
Tiracol Fort   52
Tower of
 St Augustine   90

V

Vagator   38

Published by **Landmark Publishing Ltd**
Waterloo House, 12 Compton, Ashbourne
Derbyshire DE6 1DA England

3rd Edition

ISBN 1 901 522 23 7

British Library Cataloguing in Publication Data: a catalogue record for this
book is available from the British Library.

Editor: Nicki Knott
Print: Editoriale Libraria, Trieste, Italy
Cartography: Darren Shemilt & James Allsopp
Designed by: James Allsopp

Picture Credits
All photographs have been supplied by the author

Cover Pictures
Front cover: Rajbag Beach
Back cover top: A Portuguese colonial mansion near Anjuna

DISCLAIMER
Whilst every care has been taken to ensure that the information in this
book is as accurate as possible at the time of publication, the
publishers and author accept no responsibility for any loss, injury or
inconvenience sustained by anyone using this book.